CHASM

Crossing the Divide Between Hollywood and People of Faith

Larry W. Poland, Ph.D.

NEW YORK

CHASM

Crossing the Divide Between Hollywood and People of Faith

© 2014 Larry W. Poland, Ph.D.

All rights reserved. No portion of this book may be reproduced, stored in a retrieval system, or transmitted in any form or by any means—electronic, mechanical, photocopy, recording, scanning, or other—except for brief quotations in critical reviews or articles, without the prior written permission of the publisher.

Published in New York, New York, by Morgan James Publishing. Morgan James and The Entrepreneurial Publisher are trademarks of Morgan James, LLC. www.MorganJamesPublishing.com

The Morgan James Speakers Group can bring authors to your live event. For more information or to book an event visit The Morgan James Speakers Group at www.TheMorganJamesSpeakersGroup.com.

BitLit
FOR ALL THE BOOKS YOU OWN

FREE eBook edition for your existing eReader with purchase

PRINT NAME ABOVE

For more information, instructions, restrictions, and to register your copy, go to **www.bitlit.ca/readers/register** or use your QR Reader to scan the barcode:

ISBN 978-1-63047-062-3 paperback
ISBN 978-1-63047-063-0 eBook
ISBN 978-1-63047-064-7 hardcover
Library of Congress Control Number: 2013957036

Cover Design by:
Chris Treccani
www.3dogdesign.net

In an effort to support local communities, raise awareness and funds, Morgan James Publishing donates a percentage of all book sales for the life of each book to Habitat for Humanity Peninsula and Greater Williamsburg.

Get involved today, visit
www.MorganJamesBuilds.com

Habitat
for Humanity®
Peninsula and
Greater Williamsburg
Building Partner

DEDICATION

To Bill Bright, who, in 1979, first challenged
me to make a positive spiritual investment
in the lives of those who control global media.

Blessed are the peacemakers,
for they shall be called children of God.

— Jesus of Nazareth

TABLE OF CONTENTS

CHAPTER ONE

LAYING THE FOOTERS

Solving a PR Problem

The screening room at the NBC studios in Burbank held a rather motley assortment of religious leaders from various faiths—you know, the usual minister-priest-rabbi mix. The assembly had been called together by Jay Rodriquez, NBC's Senior Vice President of Public Relations, West Coast, to help resolve a PR crisis that was driving NBC execs nuts.

The crisis was the result of a rumor that NBC was planning to air a movie in prime time near Christmas with a scene defaming Jesus Christ. Supposedly, in the opening scene of the movie, *Mary and Joseph*, a Roman soldier assaults Mary with the clear implication that Jesus is the illegitimate offspring of that union.

The fact that the rumor was not true—and never had been—didn't stop thousands of angry Christians from writing and calling the network execs with all kind of demands. The flood of rage was horrific.

Jay's plan was to call together a group of religious leaders to screen the film in advance of its air date and then have them sign a joint press release stating that the rumor was false, and the film was fine. Good strategy.

The film was fine. I watched with some anticipation of blasphemy, or at least heresy, and found none. At the end of the film, I was prepared to recommend that my boss in a Christian organization sign the press release, and I stood in line to tell Mr. Rodriquez so.

A Blast from the Reverend

In line in front of me was a young church pastor who obviously saw the film through a different filter than I did. When it came his turn to speak to the exec, he unloaded on him. He saw all kinds of unscriptural and inaccurate and even blasphemous stuff in the film and bombarded Mr. Rodriquez in a most disrespectful manner. The more he attacked Jay, the more I shrank in my shoes.

Finally, his piece having been said, the young pastor spun on his heels and exited the room in a huff. It was my turn.

I identified myself, told Mr. Rodriquez I was going to recommend support for his effort to clear NBC's name, and then got personal.

"I owe you an apology."

"How's that?" Jay replied.

"Well, I am a follower of Jesus Christ. He is the most important person in my life and has been since I was a kid, but I couldn't help overhearing what this young man said to you and the way he said it. I believe that if Jesus Christ had been in front of me in line, He would not have spoken to you as disrespectfully as this young man did. On behalf of all those people calling themselves Christians who have been angry, abusive, unkind, and disrespectful, please forgive us . . . and don't hold it against our Lord."

There was a silent three-count as Jay processed what I said, then he responded, "May I take you to lunch?"

"Sure. I never turn down a free lunch."

Thus began a journey and body of experiences stretching over more than three decades, a journey that is expressed in this book.

What Is "Hollywood?"

Let me lay a foundation for our interchange by defining terms. I'll start with "Hollywood." In reality, Hollywood doesn't exist as just a place!

What a letdown for tourists who finally make it to Hollywood and Vine or Sunset Boulevard or the Chinese Theater. I've heard them describe the sheer disappointment. They thought Hollywood's glamour was the *place*. It isn't. Hollywood isn't the shabby buildings on the boulevard lined with tourist traps, tacky lingerie stores, and greasy spoons. It's not the *place* lined with the homeless people, ladies of the evening, and druggies traversing the so-called Walk of Fame. The sign at the city limits or on the hills above the town may say "H-O-L-L-Y-W-O-O-D," but everybody knows it isn't really here. Only one major film studio is even close to the Hollywood zip code.

A day on the Universal Studios tour may give visitors a little of the magic of Hollywood and film making, but, even then, they leave knowing they let themselves be seduced by mirrors, strings, pulleys, and computer-controlled contraptions. It was a tourist *factory*. It wasn't really *Hollywood*.

A map to the "homes of the stars" is equally unfulfilling. It may feed the mystique for a tourist to imagine what—and who—lies behind those tall, iron gates and security systems on the palm-lined streets of Beverly Hills and Bel Air. But I've been in enough of them to tell you that some of them are messes and others are tacky—West Coast Gracelands. Hollywood doesn't exist there either.

A Mental Construct

Hollywood exists only in the mind. Hollywood is a *mental construct* which includes many cities—from Burbank to Manhattan, Beverly Hills to the Hamptons, Malibu to Tribeca. It's an image thing. It isn't reality, and it's slightly different in each person's mind. It's the product of pictures and sounds and celebrity stories and slick copy and publicity agent "spin" and tightly edited TV documentaries. It's the product of finely tuned media productions of Oscar and Emmy celebrations. It's the aggregate of all the films and videos and TV shows and video games and still photos and magazine articles and broadcasts and Filmland consumer products we've ever experienced—all compressed into some cranial compartment between our ears.

Show business includes many *businesses*—from video game creation to film making, from broadcasting to set storage, from premiere production to film-to-video transferring, from website design to cell phone app creation.

Hollywood includes many *products*—from DVDs to theatrical movies, from soft toys of Spiderman to Titanic wrist watches, to bras signed by sex symbols.

It includes many unique *vocations*—from limo driver to production designer, from president of network programming to on-location caterer.

It includes a whole lot of *dollars*, to be sure. With the average cost of producing a studio film somewhere around $65 million—down from $110 million before the recession—money flows.[1] But even here, the vast majority in Hollywood doesn't see much of it.

Hollywood includes many *lifestyles*—from starving actors serving tables at Hamburger Hamlet in Century City to Rodeo Drive fashion designers selling dresses for $25,000 to $100,000 a pop to car valets at the Peninsula Hotel living on tips to studio chair persons making twenty-five to one hundred million a year plus perks.

Even then, we put the cities, the businesses, the products, the vocations, the dollars, and the lifestyles all together in a pot and stir, and we don't get *Hollywood*. It all leaves us flat, like oatmeal without salt.

Deconstructing the Concept

When the "Hollywood construct" is all synthesized and processed in our minds, it still defies all the stereotypes.

- It isn't the most glamorous place on earth. In some places it's really shabby.
- It isn't the path to fame and fortune. It's the road to a lot of suffering.
- It isn't the wild, wide-open, continuing orgy of excess. You can't run multibillion dollar businesses for long stoned or dissipated.
- It isn't just a phony facade. Something has to prop up the facade.
- It isn't a dark crypt on Sunset Boulevard in which people in black robes dance around a boiling pot conspiring to steal the soul of America and the world. A conspiracy presupposes some kind of organization, and you could never *organize* Hollywood. That would be like trying to herd cats.
- There are no streets of gold. It's the same old tarmac and concrete.

"Nobody Knows Nothin'"

When Charles Fleming wrote *High Concept: Don Simpson and the Hollywood Culture of Excess*, he gave his take on Hollywood:

> From the outside, Hollywood is a mass-market fantasy factory responsible for billions of dollars in annual revenue and for America's single largest export product. It is the creator of our collective imagination, and perhaps the lasting record of what we are and believe and dream. From the outside, it is the Eldorado to thousands of young people, who every year leave small towns across the country and travel to Los Angeles dreaming of becoming the next Tom Cruise or [Angelina Jolie].
>
> From the inside, Hollywood is a shark tank, a place of desperate ambition and greed, a great, grinding soulless machine whose operators have virtually no idea what they are doing. The most forthright of them admit that they have no way of anticipating which of their movies—if any—will succeed at the box office . . .. Hollywood is a crap shoot, at best, a place where, screenwriter William Goldman has famously written, the first rule is 'Nobody knows nothin'.'[2]

Just Like a Star

A metaphor for Hollywood may be one of those stars on the Walk of Fame. There's a lot of hoopla and schmoozing on dedication day followed by long periods of nothing. A gleaming, brassy surface covering the same old dirt that lies under every other place. Shining, sparkly, and clean one day, but darkly tarnished within weeks. Framed and lighted and admired at first, then trampled under foot for decades. Dedicated to those who are kings and queens for a moment and unknown curiosities soon thereafter. When at the center of your focus, it has a distinctive beauty, but when viewed in its surroundings, it fronts for a shop selling tourist-trap knickknacks.

Finally, just like a star on the Walk of Fame, Hollywood can be *bought.*

If you do buy it, though, you still will not have purchased *Hollywood.*

Hollywood doesn't really exist . . . except in our minds.

The Hollywood Dream

But what about the Hollywood *dream?* That exists, doesn't it? Sure, in the minds of millions across the globe who have bought into the illusions that the Filmland image-makers create. But even then, the dream is illusive. It is one dream for one person and a very different dream for another. The stinger is that for all but about two percent of those who pursue their "Hollywood dream" it turns out to be a disappointment or a disaster.

As Whoopi Goldberg explains in her inimitable style, "The problem with Hollywood is that there are just too many dogs and not enough bones."[3] And most of the dogs who dream of Hollywood bones will go hungry. Hollywood is less a dream factory than it is a nightmare factory.

Then, Hollywood Is . . . What?

"Hollywood" is the aggregation of individuals who—directly or indirectly—are part of the industries which create and disseminate media product.

This includes the books, films, DVDs, TV programs, stage productions, recorded and live music, news, educational media, video games, and new media that are delivered over the internet and through personal digital assistants (PDAs) like smart phones.

You will notice that I left out professional sports, but they become an integral part of the mix through the media coverage of sporting events. Yet, professional sports generally do not fit well in the cultural milieu of Hollywood, even if NBA player Tony Parker marries *Desperate Housewives'* star Eva Longoria, or Lamar Odom marries Khloe of *The Kardashians*.

The Great Divide

Now that we have a feel for the parameters of "Hollywood," who are the people on the other side of this great gulf between the leaders of American entertainment and conservative people of faith? I express it "people of faith," because I have Conservative and Orthodox Jewish friends who are aligned on one side of the chasm with conservative Christians in many of the observations I make. At the epicenter of the Faith Community are the eighty to one hundred million "evangelical" Christians. They are a key part of the "Faith Community" and command attention if, for no other reason, than their enormous numbers.

You will notice that I will use a number of descriptive phrases to describe the "other side" of the conflict with Hollywood. The constituency is much broader than just evangelicals. I refer to it using a rather wide variety of phrases pretty much interchangeably:

    The Flyovers
    Flyover Nation
    People from the "I" States
    The Faith Community
    The Community of Faith

> The Moral Middle
> The Moral Center
> Middle America
> Moral America
> People from the Moral Middle States
> The Religious Community
> Etc.

Obviously, the above are very general, imprecise terms. Yet, defining this population with some precision is not very difficult. They are "the rest of America," those who largely do <u>not</u> buy into the worldview and cultural values of the secular, urban, postmodern, morally liberal populace which predominates in the entertainment and information industries.

The Numbers

I estimate this "Community of Faith" population as comprising about 200 million of the 312 million Americans.[4]

I reach this figure by starting with the 78.5 percent or 245 million Americans calling themselves "Christian."[5] Then, I reduce this number an arbitrary 25 percent to allow for Christians who would also call themselves "liberal," and who would be outside the value matrix of more conservative or evangelical Christians. This leaves 183.8 million.

I add to this number (1) Conservative and Orthodox Jewish adherents, (2) members of Christian "offshoot" groups such as Seventh Day Adventists, Mormons, Jehovah's Witnesses, and such, who typically share traditional Judeo-Christian core values. Then, I add (3) second-and-third generation offspring from Catholic or Protestant parents and grandparents who have no current identification as "Christian," but who have retained more conservative or even "Christian" core values. I estimate this last collection of groups at about 15 million, rounding to nearly 200 million total.

Spiritual but Not Religious

I meet people from the latter group all the time in Hollywood, many from the Catholic tradition. It is a bit sad to hear the expressions those who were raised Roman Catholic use to describe themselves when asked if they have any personal faith. You get a range of expressions like:

> I was raised Catholic, but I'm not one anymore.
> I'm a recovering Catholic.
> I'm a lapsed Catholic.
> I'm a non-practicing Catholic.
> I'm a Catholic, but I haven't been to mass in years.

Likewise, those who have jettisoned their religious roots commonly say things like:

> I'm not part of any organized religion.
> My parents were Methodist/Presbyterian/Baptist, but I left the
>   church when I went to college.
> I'm Jewish, but I'm not observant. I go only on High Holy Days.
> I'm spiritual, but I'm not religious.

There is a quiet joke around Hollywood that—at some time in the distant past—an edict was issued that Jewish media executives were required to marry Catholic wives. There are a surprising number of marriages in which this is the case. Tongue-in-cheek explanations range from "They found commonality in their shared religious guilt" to "They kept so little from their religious traditions, that they found bonding in what they *didn't* believe." Whatever the explanation, Hollywood is largely very secular. Any religious roots—and the trees and branches of religious tradition that sprang from them—have been pretty much abandoned to faraway childhood acreage.

A Non-Issue?

When Ben Stein examined the values of the entertainment community in his 1980 book, *The View from Sunset Boulevard: America as Brought to You by the People Who Make Television*, he gave one line to religion. "In Hollywood, religion is a non-Issue."[6]

Times have changed since 1980. Religion and people who are devout have become an issue. Religious belief systems have become polarizing on a score of issues sensitive to the masters of the media— from homosexuality to abortion, from the definition of marriage to sexual practices, and from respect for the "sacred" to the "born again" experience itself. The chasm between Hollywood and the Faith Community is now deeper and wider than ever before.

Few people in the more than a century of Hollywood business have made serious attempts to bridge the expanse . . . from either side. Any bridges that have been started have ended up way too short to create even any serious traffic of honest communication and good will. Typically, the power brokers on both sides have been content to lob mortar shells across the divide at selected targets and to marginalize, stereotype, assault, and slander those on the other brink.

Notice, I said, "on *both* sides." This book is not a subtle whitewashing of those from the Christian camp who have dirtied themselves by their "anger strategies" in the Hollywood/Christian warfare over the decades.

As you read this, there will be times when you will wonder just how conciliatory I am. I will be as explicit as I feel I can be in describing the zits of both the Hollywood and Faith Community camps. Hang with me to the end, and see if the two sides aren't treated with balance. That is my intent.

The mission of this book is to help both sides understand the bases for the great divide, and, through deepened understanding, become willing to reach across the breach.

It is a call for the cessation of hostilities and the building of at least one bridge of honest communication, good faith, and mutual understanding.

CHAPTER TWO

"YOU'RE WORTHLESS, AND I'M NOT"

The Conflict over Substance and Superiority

One Man's Legacy . . .

There was no way I could have known.

It was a routine visit to an exec at the Columbia Pictures studio lot in the pre-Sony days. I noticed a guy shuffling along the pavement in a work uniform with his broom and folding dustpan on a stick. I could not have known he would provide a window into the heart of Hollywood.

I watched as he wandered from candy wrapper to soft drink cup scooping various and sundry pieces of litter into his pan. He was obviously a "high mileage" person. The reddish eyes and flushed face betrayed a life enjoying way too much bubbly for his own good. His shoulders were stooped, and he looked at no one—only at the ground he had been hired to police.

As I waited for the studio shuttle to carry me to another part of the lot, I studied him. I am an obsessive student of human behavior. His affect bore an invisible sign which read, DISCOURAGEMENT. His nonverbal cues screamed "I'M NOT WORTH MUCH!" I wondered about the story behind his hiring. Was it a "mercy booking" of a different sort than is extended to has-been actors who need rent money? Was it an act of charity by some executive with a streak of compassion? He certainly would have had difficulty passing muster with the typical studio human resources department.

The man's "shuffle route" brought him near the shuttle stop where I was conducting my impromptu study. I decided to interact directly with my research subject.

"Excuse me, sir!"

He looked around as if he assumed I were talking to someone else. I stepped over to him.

"You know, you are a very important person on this lot!"

He glanced quickly from side to side, as if bewildered that this comment would be directed to him.

"I was just watching you pick up the trash and was thinking how much I appreciate what you're doing. Do you have any idea what a mess this lot would be if you weren't doing this? I just want to say 'thanks' for doing this!" I gave him a broad smile as our eyes connected.

I might as well have hooked an air hose into his backside and turned on the compressor. His chest swelled, he stood more upright, his bleary eyes brightened, and he uttered a most stunning statement, one that seemed like a *non sequitur.*

"I come from three generations of show biz' people." The announcement was delivered with not a little sense of pride.

"How terrific. Tell me about it."

"Yep, my grandfather was a limo driver who drove some of the biggest people in the business." He rattled off a short list of moguls and celebs from the twenties to the forties. I made sure he knew I was impressed.

"Then, Daddy was an extra in more than twenty movies." Again, a short list of obscure and not-so-obscure films from the fifties to the seventies.

"And here I am, working on the lot. I've been an extra in a couple of movies myself."

I oohed and aahed appropriately, and we chatted briefly until the studio shuttle arrived. I said "goodbye" and watched him head down the street between two big stages, walking a little taller and pursuing litter with what seemed to be slightly more zip. Throughout that day and over the nearly three decades since we met, his lead line has played over and over in my mind: "I come from three generations of show biz' people." "I come from three generations of show biz' people." "I come from three generations of show biz' people."

A limo driver. A movie extra. A studio litter collector. Show business.

A Contagious—and Often Terminal—Disease

He obviously had it—HIV—Hollywood Infectious Virus. This is a more-often-than-not terminal disease that distorts reality, enslaves the imagination, and sucks a person into a pattern of relationships, pursuits, and malignant perceptions that are both aggressive and inoperable.

The virus is dramatized in the oldest story in Tinseltown, an apocryphal tale of an out-of-work actor (a redundancy of sorts) who was desperate for bread money and heard that the circus was coming to town. "Circuses are entertainment," he thought to himself. So, he sought out the circus employment office. All the jobs were gone except one, and, in sheer desperation, he took it. His responsibility was to carry a big shovel and push a wheelbarrow around behind the elephants in the parade through the big top. His obvious mission was to pick up any droppings the behemoths might leave behind.

A few weeks later, a friend asked him how his job was going. "Are you kidding?" he responded, "I hate it! Can you imagine how humiliating it is to walk at the end of the parade, follow the elephants in a silly work suit, and load those enormous turds into a wheelbarrow? People laugh at me. There's no place to hide, and the stench is *awful*! It's back-breaking, too. You know how heavy that stuff is?"

"Well, if it's such a horrible job," his friend inquired, "why don't you just quit?"

"What? Are you crazy? And *leave show business?*"

Another terminal, but typical, case of HIV.

What's the source of this exaggerated importance the world puts on Hollywood, its product, and its luminaries, the view that the Tinseltown PR machine is more than happy to reinforce?

The World Would Go Right on . . .

My wife, who has a way of atomizing the smoke and mirrors on issues, said to me one day, "It's *just entertainment*! If we snapped our fingers, and it all went away instantly, the world would go on without missing a beat. We would find ways of entertaining ourselves." Sure, storytelling is essential to any culture, but we would find ways to tell our stories outside multibillion-dollar corporate machines.

Echoing a similar perspective, a veteran TV producer told me, "This is a crazy business. People get paid huge sums of money for getting up in front of a bunch of people and pretending to be somebody else." Big pay for *what?*

Yet, the prevailing notion in Hollywood and New York industry circles is that the business has some transcendent or intrinsic value. Reminds me of the story of the man in a small, rural town in the Midwest who was clearly challenged mentally. He was a sweet, cherubic man but couldn't hold a job that required any real intelligence. Finally, the town fathers decided that they needed to do something to help him make a living as an act of charity.

The decision was made to use city funds to hire him to polish the cannons on the lawn of the town hall. Faithfully, each week, the man was out there with his polish, scrub brushes, and rags. Faithfully, every two weeks, the check came to him from the town . . . and all was well.

One day, the man stepped into the office of his town employer and announced, "I'm quitting."

"You're quitting?" the supervisor asked incredulously, "What are you going to do for a living?"

"Well," the man said with pride, "I've been saving my money, and I've bought a cannon. I'm going into business for myself."

This sad tale may well illustrate the situation in the entertainment industry. Just because millions have been willing for more than a century to put huge amounts of money into supporting the "cannon polishing" of the entertainment business doesn't mean that it has any ultimate value. It surely is not weighty enough to pass the "thousand-year test"—"Will it be significant a thousand years from today?" Its messages may be, but its structures will not.

The Scary Illusion of Substance

Yet, this doesn't keep millions from . . .

- Devouring gazillions of photos and lines of copy each year about the lives and details of often-vacuous celebrities or sometimes-amoral executives, producers, and directors.
- Fawning over the faces, fashions, peccadilloes, and vanities of the Oscar and Emmy nominee crowd.

- Migrating into New York and Los Angeles seeking employ—against overwhelming odds—in some aspect of the entertainment industry's perceived "dream factory."
- Selling their souls . . . or their bodies . . . or both . . . to get a job, an acting part, a script-reading, or a 10-minute pitch meeting with a gatekeeper.
- Queuing in the wee hours of the morning—or the night before—outside the hall where award ceremonies are to be held in an effort to get a close-up look at the gods of the Red Carpet—a quasi-religious ceremony not unlike the extremes the Catholic faithful go through to kiss the ring of the pope.
- Paying obscene prices to eat at posh restaurants on the highly remote chance that some Filmland luminary might just be at a nearby table or even in a remote private room in the same establishment.

The depth and breadth of this mystique is, to me, mind-boggling.

The Global Seduction of the Mystique

What is this mystique or aphrodisiac or demonic seduction or siren's call that creates the Hollywood lure worldwide? And, worldwide it is.

As I write this, I've been in 80 countries, yet I have never been outside the seductive lure of Hollywood. I've seen chewing gum wrappers in the former Soviet Union, greasy spoon cafes in rural Kenya, and strip joints in Europe bear the name, "Hollywood."

I was once in a public washroom on the fringes of rural Siberia and was stunned to notice the hooks that were holding the two community towels on the wall—Mickey Mouse and Donald Duck. I've seen the best and worst of Hollywood's products sold in tiny kiosks in rural Ukraine along with vodka, cigarettes, and Snickers bars.

In fundamentalist Muslim countries such as those ruled by the Taliban, women may be required to be covered from head to toe with burkas, but the men still find ways to watch Hollywood movies . . . with substantially uncovered women. Even where they are officially banned, pirated videos including Hollywood's best and worst stuff flow freely in a black market. A film distributor friend wanted to test this system by *arranging* to have a feature film pirated. In no time, it was in every clandestine video store in the Muslim Middle East!

A front page story in the *L. A. Times* titled "Death to the U.S., but Not Films" described the Muslim world's love/hate relationship with our culture.[1] The chorus of anti-American sentiment which has filled the streets of the world since our response to the 9/11 atrocity is not all-encompassing. According to journalists Welkos and Yehia, the followers of Islam still flock to see American films and *love* 'em.

"Whether it's the epic tale of a doomed ocean liner in *Titanic*, the fancy swordplay of Antonio Banderas in *The Mask of Zorro*, or Julia Roberts' toothy smile in *My Best Friend's Wedding*, American movies continue to enthrall and entertain audiences in Lebanon, Syria, Malaysia and across the Islamic World."[2] Remember, too, it was U.S.-produced porn and Hollywood media product that was found in Udai Hussein's and Mommar Gaddafi's palaces when American troops raided them.

A friend who did missionary work among native American tribes inside the Arctic circle told me that the entire culture changed once satellite television hit the villages. The tribes' people dropped everything to gather around the TV and watch American TV, movies, and porn channels. It was, thereafter, a waste of time to try to hold church. They were seduced.

I love the story of a network news team in Burma tracking guerilla warriors in the jungles. Coming on a tent the journalists knew to be a guerilla field headquarters, they saw a satellite dish. Assuming the dish to be for some kind of military communication, they stepped inside only to discover the warriors watching a regional version of MTV!

Fantasyland

If someone could poll the youth of the world offering them an opportunity to come to Hollywood and become part of the film and TV industries, what percentage would jump at the chance—half or more? If the percentage were significant—as we assume it would be—the greater question is, "Why?".

Probably because this mysterious place called Hollywood bills itself as Shangri La. For a highly visible few, it offers fame, fortune, power, influence, and all the sensual pleasures of our dreams. But, the world outside Filmland doesn't know *how few* there are who really live like that, and, for that matter, how miserable many of the people are who really do!

Wandering through the set of *The Bold and the Beautiful* at CBS Television City with a senior VP of the network, I was struck by its opulence. The exec looked at me and said, "How many people really live like this? I don't." Precious few people do. But images of this opulence beamed around the world to those in two-room flats or rural farmhouses—to say nothing of grass huts and adobe hovels—are understandably seductive. Who wouldn't want to come to a place where—*it is assumed*—everybody lives like the on-screen idols, the rich, and the famous?

It is that "*it is assumed*" phrase that is the killer. The *assumptions* about Hollywood are the danger of the seduction, in large part, because they are false.

And Now a Word from the Flyovers

"The industry" is the way insiders refer to the aggregation of film, TV, and new media companies that make up the entertainment and information business. With its two U.S. centers being New York and Los Angeles, media pros refer condescendingly to those in the rest of America as "the Flyovers"—those "flown over" by the media bosses. I've also heard the masses of Americans not a part of the New York/L.A. axis referred to as "the people in Omaha" or "the People in the 'I' States." I guess that includes those from Idaho, Iowa, Illinois, and Indiana.

This elitist attitude from leaders in the industry is common and runs deep. It is hard to describe the condescension they express. Typical adjectives used include uncool, ignorant, uneducated, narrow-minded, fundamentalist, provincial, homophobic, religious right, God-and-country, rural, gun-nut, Bible thumping, right wing, and the like. Peter Bart, former editor of *Variety*, referred to evangelicals, for example, as "a bunch of know-nothing yahoos in the Bible Belt."[3] *Washington Post* journalist Michael Weisskopf wrote in a news story that followers of the Christian Right are "largely poor, uneducated, and easy to command."[4] If Weisskopf thinks that Christians of any stripe are easy to command, he's obviously never been to a church congregational meeting.

Flyovers are marked on the political map by being in the *red* (politically conservative) areas of the nation as opposed to the *blue* (politically liberal) ones. I included the word religious in the list of demeaning adjectives, because it is clear that being deeply committed to one's faith—especially in Jesus—is, to the elite, a hallmark of the unenlightened. Of course, being pro-life and believing in intelligent design rather than Darwinian explanations of origins is final proof of Flyover imbecility.

This elitism commonly comes through portrayals of the Flyovers in film and TV storytelling. The image of a bumbling, inarticulate, self-righteous, traditional-value southerner or midwesterner is pervasive. The message heard by Flyovers is a clear one: "Those of us who run media are important; you are not. We are valuable; you are not."

When veteran journalist and current Fox New Channel analyst Bernie Goldberg wrote his book, *Bias*, he noted:

> So, maybe I shouldn't have been surprised by what I heard next, but I was. Without a trace of timidity, without any apparent concern for potential consequence, Roxanne Russell, sitting at a desk inside the CBS News Washington bureau, nonchalantly referred to this conservative activist as 'Gary Bauer, the little nut from the Christian group.' *The little nut from the Christian group!* [emphasis in the original]."[5]

Goldberg noted that not a single one of the CBS News producers on the conference call where Russell slammed the Christian group gave any indication of shock or discomfort.

So, here we have the first cliff on the chasm between Hollywood and people of faith—a conflict over who is really important, over who really has substance.

Superiority Cuts Both Ways

People of faith feel superior, too. They look down on the "Hollywood crowd" as less righteous, more arrogant, out of touch, superficial, elitist, liberal, tree-hugging, amoral (or immoral), pro-homosexual, anti-family, pro-abortion, godless, faithless, unpatriotic enemies of true American (traditional) values.

Those in the Faith Community often feel the need to express their sense of moral superiority (and outrage) by crafting moralistic power-based movements like the Moral Majority, the Family Research Council, and the American Family Association to "take back America" from those awful people in the "mainstream media" and other institutions "dominated by liberals." One such movement, rooted in what is called dominion theology, views taking over the civil institutions of the world as a divine mandate in order to hasten the return of Jesus and the establishment of His earthly Kingdom. Pat Robertson's 1988 run for the U.S. Presidency was, in part, driven by this doctrine ascribed—falsely I believe—to biblical teaching.

Such power-based movements are, understandably, terrorizing to those outside the Faith Community. To them, it smacks of an effort to gain political power to enforce conservative political or conservative Christian values on those who are neither conservative nor Christian. This is viewed as the moral and political equivalent of the Taliban's gaining power and enforcing Sharia Law on the entire populace, Muslim or not.

In a conversation I had with Hollywood producer Norman Lear (who founded the People for the American Way to combat the Moral Majority), he indirectly expressed this fear. I could see his point. He indicated he didn't have a problem with evangelical Billy Graham, but he didn't share the same perspective about Pat Robertson.

I was asked to speak on the media at a Christian "Take Back America" conference. As a preamble to my talk, I made it clear that the concept was not valid in Hollywood for one very good reason—Christians never owned nor possessed Hollywood in the first place!

The Faith Community's mistrust of mainstream media is stunning. In a now somewhat dated study by Greenberg, Quinlan, and Roslan

Research, 72 percent of evangelicals felt that mainstream media were *hostile* to their moral and spiritual values, *hostile*.[6] That's nearly three out of four.

The Faith Community's view of Hollywood culture and leadership is one of nearly total disrespect. As part of contemporary culture, they follow the goings-on in Hollywood and in the lives of celebrities, but their attention is driven more by a freak-show motivation than a base of envy, admiration, or respect. They follow what happens in Hollywood from basically the same motivations as decent people who watch *The Jerry Springer Show* or pay to see the two-headed lady at the county fair.

Flyovers also tend to be scandalized when Congressional committees call on Hollywood celebrities to testify on complex issues like global warming or world hunger. They view them as not only lacking the intellectual knowledge base to speak to these issues, they view them as lacking the moral standing to do so.

Media powerbrokers are viewed as inferior, of little worth, and engaged in a business that is, at best, a waste of time and, at worst, an erosive influence on all that is good and godly.

The Fringe Factor

How did this chasm between Hollywood and the Faith Community get so deep and so wide? I believe it is, in large part, a function of what I call the "universal fringe factor."

When studying the bell-shaped curve in Statistics 101, we learned that a small percentage of data will lie two standard deviations or more from the mean . . . on both ends. If we were measuring human intelligence, presumably Albert Einstein would be in this small category at one end of the bell curve, and Alfred E. Neuman—*Mad* magazine's "What me worry?" character—on the other far end.

On the Faith Community side, we have members of the Fringe Factor who carry "God hates fags" signs and a nut or two who have shot abortion doctors or bombed abortion clinics. Then, too, since normality isn't newsworthy, the cameras and microphones usually get put in front of those who are most extreme or bizarre. Thus, the image of that entire community is created by those on the extreme ends. They get the press. They play a major role in shaping the image for the entire community.

In the Hollywood subculture, the same dynamic operates. The sex, drugs, and outrageous behavior of the Fringe Factor crowd really does not fairly represent multitudes of reasonable, decent, hardworking, "together" people who keep these multibillion dollar companies functioning and profitable.

Even those in the gay community, I believe, suffer from the Fringe Factor. I am convinced that most homosexuals and lesbians would just like to be left alone to live their lives in quiet solitude. They can't because they have this small percentage of characters who flaunt the lifestyle in outrageous ways in public, dance nearly naked in the streets on Gay Pride Days, and viciously attack those who don't support their agenda on marriage, partner benefits, and such.

Often, I have observed a person who represented himself as from my community spout something in public which was a key part of my own belief system. But the inflammatory verbiage used, the horrific matrix of attitudes projected, and the uncouth manner in which the message was delivered made me want to stuff a rag in his mouth! The Fringe Factor had struck again, and many who watched the spectacle assumed that he represented the people from my community and me.

The result: a major fault line in the chasm created greater distance between those on both sides. Both consistently marginalize the other.

CHAPTER THREE

"IT'S JUST A MOVIE!"

The Conflict over Media
Influence and Accountability

The Last Temptation of Hollywood

It was 1988, and controversy was building over reports that Universal Studios was going to release a film of Nikos Kazantzakis' book *The Last Temptation of Christ*. It was reported that an employee at Universal spirited an early version of the screenplay into the hands of Don Wildmon at the American Family Association, and the fight was on between the Faith Community and Hollywood.

Famed director Martin Scorcese was doing the film to fulfill a passion for the piece he had liked for a long time. Paramount Studios had, at one point, picked up the property, then dropped it as too hot a potato to handle, because of its controversial portrayals of Jesus and the anticipated reaction.

When a good friend, producer Tim Penland, told me the bosses at Universal had approached him about becoming a consultant on the project to build bridges with the Faith Community regarding the film, I asked the hard question. What are the probabilities that Universal is operating in good faith? We agreed that the number was low, maybe thirty percent. It turned out we were a bit generous in our estimate.

Tim said that if I would partner with him, he would sign on to the consulting gig. But as committed Christians, we agreed that if we discovered the studio was, indeed, going to release a film defaming Jesus, we would immediately terminate the relationship and work against the film's success.

After a number of requests for a script—which were met with a battery of excuses—the studio finally gave us a script which we evaluated for material which we deemed potentially offensive to the Christian community. We found eighty items on the 120-page script and rank ordered them from least to most offensive. The most offensive clearly was a dream sequence in which Jesus is shown having sex with Mary Magdalene. Horrible to imagine!

To shorten a long story, a secret call from a Universal exec made it clear to Penland and me that the Universal execs were lying to us about a lot of things. They were trying to use us (1) to hold off the dogs from the Faith Community until the film was ready for release and (2) to exploit the growing protest to sell tickets to what they knew was going to be a really tough sell at the box office.

Upon learning this, Tim quit at Universal, and we organized a press conference to reveal Universal's intentions and the content of the film. The press conference became just one small spark in what became a firestorm of reaction.

It became the greatest public protest in the history of film—before or since. More than 25,000 people gathered outside Universal in a peaceful plea to the studio not to defame Jesus by releasing the film. Studio execs turned a deaf ear and released it.

Looking back, I realized that I should have taken a lower profile in seeking to find a solution, one that would have been less confrontational to the execs involved. Also, knowing what I know now, I certainly would have written the book, *The Last Temptation of Hollywood*, with a less strident tone, one which didn't play into the anger strategy expectations of those in the industry.

This confession out of the way, I found one response from the press and from a Universal exec most stunning: "It's just a *movie!*" In essence, the Faith Community was being told, "What's the big deal? You're making a tempest in a teapot. A movie isn't significant."

Industry Doublespeak

This response was a shocker to me, because it ran so counter to the more common messages of Hollywood spin doctors about the overarching importance and global significance of every product they release.

Phrases like "This film will change your life forever," and "The world will never be the same . . ." are common to movie promotional copy. A tag line on the release of the blockbuster *Jaws* was, "You'll never go in the water again." In the case of *Last Temptation* . . . , the same execs who approve the hyperbolical language of their ad writers about the power of a single film are saying, "It's just a *movie*."? Go figure.

When this response from Universal execs was circulating in Tinseltown, a senior exec at CBS Television City heard the it's-just-a-movie line. He told me, "I hope this concept never becomes widespread; it'll kill our ad sales."

His point was that film and television—box office sales and viewership—are built on the impact of advertising. TV companies have done a superior job of convincing global business that the impact of even a thirty-second commercial—say, during the Super Bowl broadcast—could benefit a company so much that they should pay four million dollars per thirty seconds to buy the ad space! Both buyers and sellers must be agreeing on this proposition, because the ad space is usually sold. The impact of even miniscule media exposure is massive.

When Joel Siegal reviewed *The Last Temptation of Christ* for ABC's *Good Morning, America*, he unwittingly made a point for the protesters' side: "Scorcese has filled this film with images that won't be easily forgotten."[1] The Faith Community, thank you, didn't want the gross images of the film to sully forever their vision of a strong, sinless Savior. Clearly, Siegal viewed the impact as more than "just a movie."

From Undershirts to Library Cards to Reese's Pieces

It would be a waste of space to make the obvious point that even non-advertising media influence public behavior. Two legendary illustrations to make this point are not able to be confirmed. One is that undershirt sales tanked after Clark Gable took off his shirt to reveal he was wearing none in the 1934 film, *It Happened One Night*. The other is that the incidence of teenagers taking out library cards increased 500 percent after Fonzie did so in a 1977 episode of the TV series *Happy Days*. These great stories are widely accepted as fact but "unconfirmed" by Snopes.com.

But I can't resist citing at least one classic example, one even Snopes.com agrees is "true." The sale of Reese's Pieces candy went through the roof after Hershey's made a deal with Amblin Productions to use the candy in the 1982 blockbuster, *E. T.* Hershey did not pay to have Reese's Pieces used by *E. T.*, but did do an advertising tie-in after the movie's release. Within two weeks of the movie's premiere, Reese's Pieces sales exploded with reports of the increase varying from 65 percent to 300 percent.[2]

Even age-old, commonly-accepted maxims like "Monkey see; monkey do" and "The thought is father of the deed" support the power of images to influence behavior.

So, why is it again that Hollywood would say that "It's just a *movie and no big deal!*" when one of its movie scenes shows sex between Jesus and Mary Magdalene? Apparently, the 25,000 who gathered outside Universal Studios in 1988 to beg the studio not to release the film didn't see things the same way. It was a *big deal* to them.

Apparently there is a significant divide between the Faith Community and Hollywood on the influence of film and TV stories and images and their ability to affect behavior.

An Unscientific "Null Hypothesis" Experiment

In pursuing scientific research, it is common to establish what is called a "null hypothesis" at the outset. For example, if the research is exploring whether men with black hair have longer index fingers than those with blonde hair, it is convention to state it this way: "There is no relationship between hair color and index finger length in males other than that resulting from chance factors." In terms of the scientific method, this is viewed as a more objective way to begin research than by stating the hypothesis in the positive: "Men with blonde hair have shorter index fingers than those with other hair colors."

Let's take a null hypothesis approach to media influence with a short set of assumptions which can be backed by research:

- The typical American home has the TV set on 6 hours and 47 minutes a day.[3]
- Despite the movie rating system and its prohibition of R-rated films being viewed by teens, 2.5 million kids 10 to 14 have seen movies rated for older teens or adults.[4]
- Most young people watch films and videos and choose movies without much, if any, parental supervision.

Ready? See if the following null hypothesis statements resonate with you.

- There is no correlation between fashions worn by TV characters and fashions worn by American teenagers.
- There is no correlation between the words, phrases, slang, and other expressions used by film and TV characters and those used by American teenagers.
- There is no correlation between portrayals of God, faith, family, sex, political issues, and worldviews on TV and views held by youthful American viewers.
- The 20,000 30-second TV commercials typical children see each year have no influence on the thinking of those who view them.[5]
- The 8000 murders typical children will see on TV before finishing elementary school will have no influence on those children.[6]

- Viewing explicit sexual content or explicitly violent scenes will have no influence on the innocence or moral thinking of children.

You didn't get far into the list before the statements seemed absurd, did you? And that without doing any research. Some facts of life are so obvious that one does not need a high degree of either evidence or intuition to perceive them—and there is a huge body of evidence over six decades showing the link between media consumption and behavioral change.

The issue tends to rest in the hands of those gatekeepers of American media who determine what gets made into movies, TV shows, video games, and such.

How Dare You Do This to My Family and Me!

In thirty-plus years working inside the entertainment industry, I've probably seen a couple of hundred polls on what Americans think about the influence of Hollywood on the culture, on sexuality, on faith, on family, and on violent behavior. I have never seen a poll in which respondents viewed Hollywood's influence as positive. In fact, I have never seen numbers under 70 percent negative, and those numbers have run as high as 93 percent.

The anger among the Flyovers—especially people of faith—is particularly strong. Speaking in hundreds of Faith Community settings across America, I discover a level of anger that is particularly intense. Here is a sampling of the questions I get:

- "Why do they produce such awful stuff?"
- "Don't they care what they are doing to our kids . . . nation . . . culture?"
- "Are there no decent people out there in Hollywood?"
- "Is there some kind of conspiracy to destroy our faith/values/families?"
- "Will they produce *anything* that makes a buck?"

When I endeavor to tell them that there are a lot of very fine, principled people in media leadership, I have a herculean time selling it. When I explain that our organization has a data base of more than

4000 very committed Christian people of faith who work in the industry, they are incredulous. "Then, if there are these fine people, why doesn't it show? I have a hard time finding a movie or TV series to watch any more."

Coping Strategies

The ire has increased dramatically since the beginning of the movie industry at the start of the last century. As times and the industry have changed, the coping strategies of the Faith Community have changed. They have been desperate to protect themselves from Hollywood's increasingly erosive influence. So, they have tried the following:

1. Isolate and Condemn 1900-1950

When I grew up, the approach to Hollywood among the most conservative in the Faith Community was what I call the *isolate and condemn strategy*. Basically, this approach made going to a movie a sin—even if the movie was wholesome—because it was supporting a godless industry.

This strategy kept kids like me from going to movies—except for wholesome Disney films like *Bambi* or *Song of the South* and rare redemptive films like *Ben Hur, The Ten Commandments,* and *The Greatest Story Ever Told.* In these cases, the lure of the film caused a lot of church folks to "rise above principle" and see the film. Even then, we parked down the street, came a little late, left a little early, and sat in the back of the theater! It had the same "sinful feel" to it as sneaking into a burlesque show.

2. Separate but Equal 1950-1970

The "isolate and condemn" strategy worked pretty well, until Hollywood came into our homes in the forties via television. Now, the folks who made movies and radio were also making television. The net result was that the bad stuff was no longer downtown, it was downstairs.

Time for a new strategy. In a twist of if-you-can't-beat-'em-join-'em, the Faith Community apparently had this epiphany that maybe film and TV could be used for righteous purposes as well as nefarious ones. Thus, was born the *separate-but-equal* strategy.

I remember the message well, "The devil has had control of films and television for way too long. It's time for *Christian* films and *Christian* TV." The Billy Graham Evangelistic Association was one of the first to launch into making films with explicitly Christian messages. They bought a nice little studio in Burbank, founded Worldwide Pictures, and began making movies to advance their cause. The films commonly had a Billy Graham Crusade written into the story line near the end at which the main characters walked the aisle and were born again. Not being able to get conventional distribution into theaters, they "bought out" or "four-walled" theaters for a showing and got local churches to sponsor their fare.

The Christian movie idea gathered incredible momentum. In a decade or so, Billy Zeoli was heading Gospel Films, Inc., and the company was distributing and renting from a huge catalog of films made by people of faith for people of faith. When a pastor wanted a break from message preparation for the Sunday evening service—or a little extra sizzle to promote the same—he would rent a Christian film and show it for the folks. I remember that services featuring a movie had a distinctly bigger draw than those in which the preacher preached!

This move to get into the production of films was built on an already growing body of radio preachers and radio stations owned by nonprofit organizations which still exist today. Most don't realize the strength of about 2400 Christian radio stations and 100 full-power Christian TV stations across America.[7] Most of the content delivered is "family-friendly," decidedly Christian, skewed heavily toward the conservative community, and has either contemporary Christian music or preacher/talk formats. The National Religious Broadcasters (NRB) has gained tremendous political strength representing the interests of these stations and their huge constituency of evangelicals.

Then, the advent of the contemporary Christian music (CCM) industry created a windfall of financial and influence opportunities for people of faith. Now the second most popular music format on radio, CCM is a major factor in the Christian separate-but-equal strategy.[8]

But by its very definition, the separate-but-equal strategy really hasn't insulated the Faith Community from the ubiquitous influence of Hollywood. And it certainly hasn't effected any measurable change on the multibillion dollar "secular" entertainment megacorporations.

3. Anger Strategies 1970-2000

By the seventies, things in Hollywood had gotten out of control from the view of the Flyovers and the Faith Community. Moral restraints of the Catholic and Protestant organizations which, earlier, had monitored and consulted with studios on the content of films, were largely gone or impotent. Moviemaking was no longer the province of six or eight major studios. The rise of independent film production companies had made the task of monitoring or exercising any content influence virtually impossible. The animals were now running the zoo.

In the meantime, the gay rights movement was picking up steam, and gays and lesbians were becoming more and more influential in Hollywood. I had a senior exec at NBC tell me in the early eighties, "If we air anything that reflects negatively on the gay lifestyle, I have two or three prominent members of the gay community in my office within 72 hours to hold us accountable, and to try to make sure it doesn't happen again." A wise strategy. Gay strategies were so effective, in fact, that it became almost obligatory that dramas and sitcoms have at least one lovable, witty, and otherwise attractive gay character, or the series wouldn't sell to the networks.

Then, by the seventies, the moral liberals were completely in control of the industry. So-called "traditional values" were being trashed in story lines as a matter of course. Free sexual involvement from teens to marrieds was common. Sitcoms were becoming more and more mean-spirited. Folks like writer/producer Steven Bochco of *Hill Street Blues* and *NYPD Blue* fame were openly trying to overthrow the network broadcast standards departments complaining that TV should allow content like R-rated movies. Bochco was giving NBC's Broadcast Standards execs fits and was proud of it.

The Flyovers—and especially the Moral Conservatives—had had enough. So, they ushered in the era of boycotts, protests, and hate mail. Million-person mailing lists were soon leveraged by Christian protest organizations (sounds a bit oxymoronic to me) to send protest cards, letters, and petitions, and to support boycotts of ABC or XYZ. Of course, the call to protest and boycott always included a fiery fund letter and a postage-paid envelope for donations.

The problem wasn't that the Faith Community was responding to the flood of offensive material. It has the right and privilege of expressing concerns like any other segment of the society. The problem was the often vicious and hate-filled attitudes and comments shared. Even "selective patronage" in keeping with one's values is appropriate, but the warlike approach to company boycotts was the issue.

Skeptical of the success of these efforts, I told friends I would know that the 1997-2005 Southern Baptist boycott of Disney/ABC was successful when there wasn't a Baptist man in America who would watch *Monday Night Football*, because it was aired by ABC. Of course, the boycott failed. A boycott against a local video store might succeed, because the owner draws his business from a small radius around the store. But Disney/ABC? C'mon. You can fence a pond, but you can't fence an ocean.

Worse than that, the anger strategies generated generations of ill will toward Christians. In a ten-minute cold call on the head of a New York media company, I finished my eight-minute presentation offering our consulting services and asked for a response.

"You're not angry, are you?"

"No, I'm not angry. I'm not trying to spoil your day. I'd like to help you. You have a tougher job than I have."

"It's so refreshing to meet somebody who's not angry. Everybody's angry any more." It was clear that meeting a Christian who wasn't angry was a stunning, but welcome, departure from what he had been conditioned to expect.

Three Failed Strategies

I sat in the office of a VP for Public Relations at NBC and he announced, "We got 250,000 letters from [Christian protest organization] this week. The mail room is full of bags of mail."

"Talk to me," I said, "how much does that influence NBC?"

"Aw, not much."

"Not much? That's a quarter of a million people who took the time to communicate on the issue. How 'not much'?"

"Larry, it's a fund raiser. Send your money to us and this tear-off card to NBC. We got one letter 250,000 times. We know what they are doing. We subscribe to their stuff."

Here you had it, three strategies that were ineffective in changing the way things were in Hollywood and the kind of product coming out of the place. A friend inside the power structure of Disney/ABC during the Southern Baptist boycott told me that then-chairman Michael Eisner scoffed at the threats and cynically read the worst examples of the hate mail they received in executive meetings.

The Spot-on-the-Wall Factor

To be honest, most Christian wrath is reflective of what I call the spot-on-the-wall factor. You can walk into a beautifully appointed, richly decorated and immaculately cleaned room with one filthy, dark smudge on the wall. You see only the dark spot. So it is with the guide to TV programming that comes in your newspaper or on screen. I've challenged my friends to go through that guide and circle only the programs that offend them or their Christian values. Usually, the portion of such programs is ten percent or less, but that is not the point. The dark spot is so much more visible, so much uglier, and so deeply offensive that it blinds the viewer to the rest of the beauty of the room.

So What about Accountability?

In three decades of attending media trade conferences, I've sat through scores of panel discussions in which heads of studios, cable companies, and networks are asked to opine on everything from whether telecoms or satellite content providers are going to take over the industry to whether reality shows are the salvation of or a curse to television.

In three—only three—panels has any question been directed to the gatekeepers regarding personal responsibility for the content they take public. In two of the incidents, the question was so oblique and the response so rushed as to barely warrant mentioning. In the third, as I recall, the moderator was Chris Mathews. As a wrap-up question, he asked something like, "Sometimes, as I am watching some of the stuff that is aired—and I have kids—I wonder, do you ever stay awake nights wondering if you are doing the right thing by some of this programming?"

Same old, same old. In all three—and especially in this third situation in which the question was very direct, and each panelist had to weigh in—we were told:

- "We have to have something for everybody. I don't like some of the stuff we air, but people are different and have different tastes."
- "People talk about too much violence; there's more violence on the evening news . . . and ours is make believe."
- "We just give people what they want; we don't determine what that is."
- "If there isn't a demand for it, we don't air it."
- "This is a First Amendment issue. In this country, we have free speech, and that includes the freedom to air what people want."
- "We're criticized for too much sex. Yet, there are commercials that warn against the side effects of a four-hour erection."
- "Every TV has an 'off' button; if they don't like it, they don't have to watch it."

According to *Variety*, ABC News correspondent Jeff Greenfield used his keynote speech to the National Association of Broadcasters convention one year to condemn TV talk shows and tabloid television. While he defended TV as not responsible for the ills in society, he admitted that TV's critics have a right to question TV's role in society when they air talk shows that are "a parade of dysfunctional horrors and leering hosts and audiences who were last seen crowding around the guillotine in Paris 200 years ago." He noted the industry "shouldn't be puzzled as to why so many people think TV has made the country worse off."[9]

Hitting TV executives, Greenfield assaulted the flaky reasons they give for producing and airing these shows, rationalizations such as "People want to see these programs," and "It's the marketplace in action." He concluded soberly, "Just sit back one afternoon and turn on the set, and realize that what you are seeing is a result of the deliberate, conscious decisions of some of the most powerful, respected people in this business . . . ."[10]

Dirty Little Secret

Jeff missed another compelling point. The dirty little secret is that some of the nicest, most-principled men and women in American industry head companies like Cox, Comcast, Charter, Cablevision, Dish, Direct TV, and telecoms like AT&T and Verizon. I know. I've met most of them. Yet, they deliver the hardest of hard-core pornography to millions around the globe through Pay Per View, collect the revenue from this addictive debauchery, and, apparently, sleep well at night.

A top exec at AT&T who was a devout Catholic told me, "When I took this job, I had no idea I'd be asked to decide what level of pornography we would carry, level 1, level 2, or level 3." He went on to explain that level 1 was airbrushed nudes, level 2 was explicit heterosexual sex, and level 3 was gay sex, group sex and everything worse. "Fortunately, our chairman opted for nothing worse than level 2. I hate it, but we knew we were losing subscribers to companies who carried porn, and our stockholders would miss the thirty percent of our revenue."

It is a deep mystery to me how programming impact from what is arguably the most powerful medium in the history of mankind to influence, inspire, manipulate, inform, seduce, instruct, pollute, motivate, and deceive the human race can be brushed off when it comes to personal responsibility. Believe me, the leaders of media know its power . . . and how to use it.

This is what gets the Flyovers crazy—seemingly no sense of accountability on the part of the leadership in media. I liken it to, say, Wonder Widget, Inc. (WWI). Research has shown that millions of people have been injured by defective WWI widgets. A Congressional investigation ensues. The execs at WWI are hauled into court and issued Cease and Desist Orders, assessed huge fines, or put in the slammer. Gazillion dollar class action lawsuits are filed against WWI with billion dollar judgments for the plaintiffs. It's called *product liability.*

Not in media. Apparently, to industry leaders, the stuff they put out is "just a movie" when it serves their purposes to say so.

CHAPTER FOUR

"WHAT DO YOU MEAN, IT'S WRONG?"

The Conflict over the Nature of Good and Evil

Scandal Power

Actor Cliff Robertson had a dilemma in February, 1977. The IRS notified him that he had tax responsibility for $10,000 he had received from Columbia Pictures, but Cliff had no recollection or record of ever seeing the money.[1] His accountant confirmed that the money had not been received and then notified the bean counters at Columbia. They said that the check had indeed been issued and provided a copy of the endorsed instrument.

Voilà, the check *had* been signed and cashed, but it was not Cliff's signature! A real life whodunit was now in play. Probably some low-life thief in the studio accounting department or mail room, right? After the Los Angeles Police Department and the FBI investigated, the culprit turned out to be none other than David Begelman, the chairman of Columbia Pictures!

Begelman was sentenced to community service for forgery, but an internal investigation by the studio discovered that this was the tip of the Begelman graft iceberg. He had embezzled an additional $65,000 on forged checks, had improvements made at his home on studio funds, and more. He was a felon, guilty of grand larceny.

At this point, the story becomes surreal. So surreal, in fact, that David McClintock, a *Wall Street Journal* investigative journalist, wrote a best-selling book on the scandal titled *Indecent Exposure: A True Story of Hollywood and Wall Street.*[2]

As it turned out, the greater scandal was the way the board of directors of Columbia handled Begelman. They reinstated him! A fight ensued among the directors over the matter with a number wanting to keep a convicted felon on as studio chairman!

Finally, bowing to public pressure, the board fired him and hired a squeaky clean Brit, David Puttnam, to take his place and clean up the image and operations of the studio. Puttnam was the producer of *Chariots of Fire*, you may recall. Puttnam lasted fewer than two years before he bailed. His parting comments indicated that the culture of corruption (not his words) was more than he could handle. He went back to England with less than complimentary things to say about the ethics and character of the film business in Hollywood.

Should you think that this corruption was an anomaly at Columbia, Nancy Griffin and Kim Masters wrote a later book on the maniacal reign of Sony/Columbia's co-chairmen titled, *Hit and Run: How Jon Peters and Peter Guber Took Sony for a Ride.*[3]

It would be unfair to paint all of Hollywood with the Columbia brush, but undeniably the culture of the film and TV business is not in phase with the more ethically based business culture of Flyover Nation. Those in the heartland of the U.S. shake their head in wonderment when they read of the goings-on in Studioland.

Wanted: Lie Detectors

It is a basic operational principle in Middle America that you tell the truth. It is a pleasant surprise when I return to the "I" State in which I grew up to discover how much business is done on a handshake. There, even banking operates with a matrix of "truth expectation." Not so in Hollywood.

In 2002, the *Los Angeles Times* launched a series on the ethics of Hollywood in Column One of the front page.[4] The first column was titled, "Inhale. Lie. Exhale. Lie." Written by David Shaw, the thesis of the piece was that "in Hollywood, lying is a way of life." Anita Busch, Editor of the *Hollywood Reporter*, said, "If I talk to 100 people in a day, 99 of them are lying, and the other one is my mom."[5]

The article chronicled how industry people lie about money, lie about box office numbers, lie about other people, and even try to get journalists to lie for them. I heard of a conversation in a Beverly Hills hotel or restaurant in which one man screamed, "You are lying to me!" The other responded, "I know, but hear me out."

Patrick Goldstein, a movie reporter for the *L. A. Times* explains:

> Look, you call a movie executive who spent the morning talking to people about how to turn the nurse who's the hero [sic] in a book he just bought into a fighter pilot for a movie version. Then, he was on the phone trying to get financing from a German company by telling them the movie will cost $40 million, when he knows it will cost at least $75 million. Then, he's telling someone at the studio that his latest movie had a test-screen score of 90, when it was really 65. Then, you call him, as a reporter, and you expect him to tell you the truth?[6]

I Won't Lie for You

I have a friend who went to work for a legendary Hollywood talent agency. She noticed that, periodically, a secretary would go screaming and cursing out of the place, quitting because she could no longer work for one out-of-control agent. After yet one more secretary exited, human resources called her in and asked if she would take the position as assistant to this agent.

She said, "Let me think about it over the weekend." She had recently come to faith in Jesus Christ and, even before that, had Flyover values and integrity. "Think about it" was code for "pray about it." After praying, she felt God wanted her to take the job, so she did.

She immediately noticed that the agent lied about everything. She told me, "He lies even when there is no reason to lie." One day early in the job, a call came in for the agent, and she asked the caller to hold. She buzzed the agent and identified the caller.

"Tell him I'm out of town."

My friend told the caller, "I'm sorry. Let me keep you on hold a minute more." She strode into the office and said, "Look Mr. [last name], I'm going to do my best to work hard for you, serve you, and make you a success. There is just one thing I won't do. I won't lie for you. I'm putting the call through."

Stunned, the agent accepted the call. Ten years later, the assistant was still in her job, and the boss trusted her so much he had made her a cosignatory on all of his bank accounts!

The agent was so stunned to find unshakable character that he kept her for ten years, not ten weeks! She remained his counsel and cosignatory even after she left the job.

Lies by Profession

In Hollywood, not only is lying common, a lot of professional people make good money doing it for a living. In Dennis McDougal's book *The Last Mogul,* an unauthorized biography of MCA/Universal's longtime boss Lew Wasserman, the story is told of Lew's career as a spin doctor and agent.[7]

Joan Bennett, a raven-haired beauty and film star since the silent era, was married to a fiery independent producer named Walter Wanger. While Wanger had his life of infidelity, he wanted his adultery to be one-sided. When Bennett began slipping away for trysts with her lovers, Wanger went ballistic, hired a private detective to catch her in the act, and branded her a whore.

In an affair with her agent, Jennings Lang, Joan Bennett lied saying that Lang was just a patient listener to the story of her troubled marriage—nothing more.

As she and Lang returned to her car from a rendezvous one afternoon in 1951, Wanger suddenly appeared, argued with the two vociferously, and then put a bullet in Lang's leg with a pistol. When the police arrived, neither would press charges, and Wasserman's PR team sprang into action telling reporters that "Wanger was distraught over financial reversals, bringing on delusions that his wife was having an affair." Professional lies.

Cinematic Lies

In Hollywood, the lying doesn't just permeate the system, it is common to its product. Movies lie.

Naturally, I'm not talking about fictional movie plots. Of course, they are made up. I'm talking about treatments of actual historical events in which there is full documentation to support the facts of the story. I'm not even talking about taking "creative license" by filling in gaps where the facts of the story are in doubt. I'm describing *outright falsification* of the facts, message, motivations, and outcomes of an actual historical event.

It's been called "revisionism," the altering of the facts of a story or of historical evidence in order to make the message of a movie very different from reality.

One of the best revisionist filmmakers is Oliver Stone. His revisionism in films like *Good Morning, Vietnam* and *JFK* are hallmarks of the revisionist's art. Anyone who served in Vietnam and saw his Nam films is scandalized by the misrepresentations. I remember laughing out loud in a New York theater watching *JFK* as Stone used tear-stirring scenes to fill in gaps in the evidence for his argument that, among other things, Lyndon Johnson was an accomplice to John Kennedy's assassination. It was masterful . . . and false.

But the practice didn't begin with Stone. Director Stanley Kramer's 1960 film *Inherit the Wind*, is a classic piece of cinematic prevarication.[8] Starring Spencer Tracy, Frederic March, and Gene Kelly, the movie is based on a real-life case in 1925 involving lawyers Clarence Darrow and Williams Jennings Bryan. The movie centers on the case against a science teacher accused of the "crime" of teaching evolution in the classroom. Even a cursory reading of original court transcripts and contemporary news coverage reveals the movie version to be a major fabrication. That there was an agenda in the revisionism is without debate. The story was altered to make Bryan and his "fundamentalist" cohorts look like rubes and the suave Clarence Darrow and his arguments impressive and intellectual. Science "wins one" over fundamentalist faith in a court of law, not in truth, but in the movie.

For the majority of the American populace who still reveres "You shall not bear false witness" as a divine command, Hollywood lying is anathema . . . and insulting. It is also evil.

@&$%**# Language

Talk radio host and film critic/historian Michael Medved made a striking point in a review of a Hollywood film that was laced throughout with obscenities and profanities. In making the point that the filthy language was totally unnecessary to good film making, he said, "I've never heard anyone come out of a theater saying, 'You know, that would have been a great film, if only it had had a few more 'F' words.'"[9]

While I credit MTV and its various partner channels for using the "bleep" mechanism to keep the actual foul language from being heard by their TV viewers, I have often wondered two things. One, can they find no higher quality young people to feature in their shows—ones whose speech is more respectable and would provide better role models for young viewers? Two, did it ever occur to them that the context of the "bleeps" makes most of the words totally discernible to viewers anyway? Of course it did. But the bleep-bleep-bleeps continue, and they improve the virtue of the shows precious little.

For the above reason (and others) people of faith in America who police what their kids watch listed MTV as the number one TV channel they forbid. In research commissioned by my organization, Mastermedia International, polling by America's Research Group (ARG) showed that nearly half (49%) of the restrictive parents forbade their kids from viewing MTV.[10]

I'm stunned by the creativity of some of the folks I overhear in public in the way they can make the "F" word into a noun, an adjective, an adverb, and an expletive as well as a verb. Equally fascinating is the manner in which some can find a way to jam three or more uses of this one word into a single sentence or eight to ten uses in a single paragraph! What isn't creative is the disuse of all the other words that could be used instead. The Second Edition of the 20-volume *Oxford English Dictionary* contains full entries for 171,476 words in current use, and 47,156 obsolete words. To this, may be added around 9,500 derivative words included as subentries.[11] Certainly one or more of 228,132 words could be found to substitute for the "F" word!

The deterioration of public speech and the inclusion of unprintable, barbaric, sexually explicit words and phrases in common parlance is a prime mark of the deterioration of our culture . . . led by Hollywood. Film and television bear some responsibility for the common acceptance of this degraded language.

We are what we speak. Jesus explained, "For out of the overflow of his heart a man speaks."[12] The mouth is a window to the soul, and a clean heart does not spew forth filthy or destructive language any more than an evil heart is capable of expressing genuinely pure, loving, upbuilding communication. Could it be that the absence of personal spiritual redemption in the media community is the root cause of the flood of verbal sewage that comes out of their mouths and is recorded in their scripts and productions?

I've heard Hollywood writers defend the inclusion of awful language as necessary to make the characters "authentic." "You can't have scuzzy characters using nice language" is the argument. Granted, to a point. But, I have two responses to the argument. The first is that there are more ways to portray evil in a character than just by the words spoken. One of the more evil characters in film is Darth Vader from the *Star Wars* series. No one missed the point that this is one supremely bad dude. Yet, he used language that, except for a "hell" or "damn," was not an embarrassment to parents who took their kids to the films.

"Authenticity"

My second argument comes from an incident involving one of our organization's consulting staff. He was invited by execs at HBO to a nice dinner in New York celebrating the launch of the miniseries *Band of Brothers*. HBO also invited some surviving soldiers from World War II, men who had lived the scenes captured in the miniseries. After screening a portion of the series for the dinner guests, one of the octogenarian soldiers was asked to speak and indicate whether the filmmakers had captured the true essence of life on the battlefield at that time.

The veteran assured those attending that the producer and director had, indeed, recreated the way things were in those horrific, bloody battle scenes. "But," the man said, "the language was not accurate. We were not permitted to use foul language like that. Our commanders wouldn't allow it." So much for "authenticity."

Walk the halls of any public high school or middle school in America, and the language will sound like the sound track from an expletive-laced Hollywood film. Flyover parents don't appreciate it. People of faith are incensed. They have enough challenge getting their teenagers to use respectful, publicly acceptable, pure language without horrific speech being modeled by their kids' screen stars.

This is especially true for two of the most common phrases, "Oh, my God," and "Jeeesus Chriiist." Both are as offensive to those of the Christian faith as the "N" word to African Americans and violate one of the Big Ten Commandments: "You shall not misuse the name of the Lord your God."

People from Flyover Land ask me, "Why do they put so much foul language in movies and on TV?" My answer: "A lot of Hollywood leaders talk that way . . ., and I guess they think everyone else does, too." I heard a person use the "F" word in a tribute to very devout Hollywood producer at her memorial service. I was glad the deceased wasn't present to hear it.

The chasm between Hollywood speech and speech of the moral masses is huge.

Sex Is Beautiful . . . or Is It?

I know what you may be thinking: "Oh, boy, here it comes. The Puritans are alive and well. We're going to get preached to about sex." Not really, but a major gulf between Middle American morality and Hollywood's is over sex. Hugh Hefner of Playboy refers to people critical of his wide open practice of sex with many partners as "fun-hating fundamentalists." This is hardly an accurate description of those who are out of phase with the prevailing view of sex in Hollywood. Furthermore, not to treat the subject would be to ignore the proverbial 600-pound gorilla in the parlor.

One of the last articles author C. S. Lewis wrote was one published in *The Saturday Evening Post*, December 21-28, 1963, shortly after his death. It was titled, "We Have No Right to Happiness." In it, Lewis examines the notion expressed in the American Declaration of Independence of an "unalienable right" to the "pursuit of happiness" and its misapplication to the thinking of current generations.

The article starts with Lewis relating a conversation he overheard at a restaurant in which a woman named Clare justifies another woman's divorce and remarriage on the premise, "She had a right to happiness." The man she married also divorced his spouse to marry, and, presumably, he expected the action would bring happiness to him, as well. The two were decidedly <u>un</u>happy with their previous mates.

Without getting into the powerful arguments Lewis sets forth to demonstrate the lunacy of declaring a "right" to something that depends on so many factors beyond our control, I want to highlight one comment Lewis made about Clare.

> For one thing, I believe that Clare, when she says 'happiness,' means simply and solely 'sexual happiness.' Partly because women like Clare never use the word 'happiness' in any other sense. But, also, because I never heard Clare talk about the 'right' to any other kind . . . .. Every unkindness and breach of faith seems to be condoned provided that the object aimed at is 'four bare legs in bed.'[13]

The line is now drawn for this argument. In much of Hollywood, "four (or more) bare legs in a bed" is a prime value, one that transcends a lot of values people outside the San Fernando Valley and Manhattan think are exponentially more important.

A Shocking Question

A friend of our organization is a lovely and talented professional in Hollywood. As she worked out regularly at a local health club, she noticed a middle aged man observing her. In the course of time, he introduced himself, and the two spoke casually from time to time at the club. She discovered him to be the head of one of the major movie studios.

Then, one day, he "popped his question" to her. With no apparent hesitancy or embarrassment, he asked, "Do you date married men?"

The sheer audacity of such a question in Flyover country would stun the hearer, as it did this deeply devout Christian woman in Hollywood. In Hollywood, however, the question could be delivered without apology or embarrassment.

I mentioned to a senior VP at a major television network that I had learned through a highly unusual source that the network head was having an affair. His response, somewhat matter-of-factly, was "at least one."

I could provide a list of venerated Hollywood legends whose public persona is "happily married," but who have one or more "kept women" as mistresses and have had them for years. Lest there be any mistake, Hollywood women have their dalliances as well.

The husband of a legendary film star brought his lovers into their own home through a back entrance for twenty years with his wife's knowledge and disapproval.

Are these examples typical of all those with success in media? Of course not. But they're a whole lot more common in Movieland than in the heartland.

A Long-Forgotten Concept

Parents in the heartland are equally scandalized by Hollywood immodesty. They don't respect it in the films and lives of celebs, on one hand, and they see the effect it is having on their children on the other. I wonder if the typical person from the Screenland culture would even have a functional definition of the word "modesty." It is a long-forgotten concept.

Suppose, in Flyover country, a woman showed up at a local event wearing a see-through dress without a stitch of clothing under it, as more than a handful of celebs have appeared at award ceremonies. Suppose a woman posed for the local newspaper topless or nude (as if a local paper would print it anyway) as so many have in Hollywood. Suppose a man singing at a local Kiwanis Club talent show grabbed his genitals like pop singers and music video performers do. Suppose that one of the leading socialites in a "red state" community intentionally leaked a "sex tape," so that the world could see it. In which of the above cases would the action enhance the respect and image of the person and "advance their careers?" No answer necessary. Yet, these things happen in the media world, and their peers think this is cool or no big deal.

When it comes to the impact of this immodesty on Middle America's youth, it is scary. How many a mom has seen her daughter heading out of the house and said, "You are going out in public dressed like *that?*" Or how many dads have been chagrined to hear their wives say, "We couldn't find a prom dress. All they sell is stuff that makes girls look like prostitutes." Where did these styles and actions come from? I'll let you guess.

What Rules?

Why this radical difference in values toward sex and modesty between the real America and Hollywood? I've pondered this question for years. I think that Brad Pitt answered the question well in 2001 soon after he became a star and before he was, himself, reshaped by the industry's warped values. In a *New York Times* article, Brad commented on the impact of celebrity on him and others. He observed,

We can get away with things that other people can't, and you start to believe the lie that you are special, that you're better than other people. You start demanding that kind of treatment. Most of the time, I fight it, because I know I'm going to get older, and it's going to go away, but at times I succumb to it.[14]

In essence, the Hollywood luminaries are socialized into a system that says when you get to be "big" in the industry, the rules no longer apply to you. You can do what you want.

Country Western singer Brad Paisley nailed it in his spoof on being a celebrity:

I'll get to cry to Barbara Walters,
When things don't go my way.
An' I'll get community service,
No matter which law I break.

I'll make the supermarket tabloids,
They'll write some awful stuff.
But the more they run my name down,
The more my price goes up.

Cuz, when you're a celebrity, it's adiós reality.
No matter what ya do;
People think you're cool, just 'cause you're on TV.[15]

Not in Our Home Town

Rare are these illusions of immunity from the consequences of behavior among the *real* people of America. With few exceptions, they know the rules of God and man apply to them, and they live with this matrix of understanding. They know the rules of sex, marriage, covenant, loyalty, fidelity, purity, and unconditional love apply and are non-negotiable. They believe, as theologian E. Stanley Jones once said, "Nobody ever really breaks God's laws; you challenge them, and they break you."[16]

This "rules-don't-apply-to-me" factor is compounded by the fact that the spiritual worldview of most in Hollywood doesn't consider God or His rules at all. This view may be a consequence of one or more of the following:

- Darwinian beliefs that we are all here as the result of chance factors; no divine plan nor creator, thus, no divine law nor accountability
- Adherence to a religion that has rules-are-relative beliefs such as: "I am God," or "God is within me," not outside holding me accountable
- A kind of Epicureanism that preaches "You only live once," so grab all the sensual gusto you can without reference to rules or consequences
- Sheer narcissism in which "The galaxy spins around me" and "Nothing and no one will stand in the way of my getting my every whim satisfied."
- Seduction into the culture through such powerful peer pressure that the consequences of behavior are totally obscured

Not one of the above five factors is common in the Red States. In fact, the Hollywood style of sexual license which tolerates marital infidelity, same-sex intimacy, philandering men, loose women, man-boy-love, transgender behavior, bisexual intimacy, and no-holds-barred pornography is viewed as wrong . . . sin . . . evil. Once more, the prohibition of sex outside of a covenant commitment in heterosexual marriage is one of the "Big Ten" divine commandments for all of those in the Judeo-Christian tradition.

This gap between Hollywood and conservative America is so wide on basic definitions of right and wrong, good and evil, that there is no span I know of that can bridge it short of widespread spiritual redemption.

CHAPTER FIVE

THE BILLY MAHER EVANGELISTIC ASSOCIATION

The Conflict over the Value of God and Faith

The Launch of a Crusade

I sat in the nearly empty multiplex theater with my pen and pad in hand tracking through a documentary of the most absurd of the planet's religious behavior. I tried to ignore the language and tone of mean-spiritedness that inevitably seeps through his stuff, but Bill Maher scored some really strong points with me in his film *Religulous (2008)*—a combination of the words "religion" and "ridiculous." The name states his thesis—all of religion and religious thinking is without merit and totally ridiculous.[1]

I like Bill Maher. He is bright, witty, and thinks for himself. He'd be better served in his humor and his worldview, if his root of psychological and spiritual bitterness were extracted. But that doesn't keep him from saying some things that need to be heard.

As *Religulous* led me through cinematic portrayals of the worst nonsense in the world of belief, at points, I cheered. Bill is right about a lot of things, especially when he takes on "religion." I'm not a fan of *religion*. I've been in 80 nations and have seen about every form of religious stuff imaginable, including a huge variety which an encyclopedia would list under Christianity. Not impressed. In fact, I'm not sure I'd recommend a trusted friend attend a lot of establishments listed in the Yellow Pages under "church." For my money, religion is man's attempt to reach God or, in some cases, create one. I'm into a spiritual *relationship*, a personal faith in a personal God who has made my life meaningful and complete—a relationship that can function with or without "organized religion." Maher didn't deal with a God-man *relationship*. It's likely he hasn't experienced that.

And Now, the Sermon

The element of Bill Maher's film that was most fascinating to me was his sermon at the end. For what seemed like five minutes, Bill gave a sermon and even an "altar call." He called viewers to come to faith in his premise that religion is futile and often destructive, and God doesn't exist. He noted that about six percent of Americans do not believe in a higher power or God. He called for the six percent to unite, organize, and mobilize to eliminate the scourge of religion from our planet. The only thing missing from his own version of a Billy Graham film was George Beverly Shea singing "Just As I Am" and throngs moving to the front of the theater to repent. There, right at the end of his film, it happened. The Billy Maher Evangelistic Association (BMEA) was launched.

Evangelist he is. While Bill is certainly very "out there" with his views and his rhetoric, I believe he has thousands of quiet sympathizers who run much of media—sympathizers who are likely recruits for the BMEA. While they are not open, avowed atheists like Bill, they are "practicing atheists."

Even Madalyn Murray O'Hair, the famed atheist spokesperson and activist, was smart enough to redefine an atheist. She did not use the familiar, "An atheist is a person who does not believe in God or in the existence of God." I heard her on NBC's *The Tonight Show* decades ago define an atheist as "One who orders his life as if there is no God." That's convenient. America and Hollywood are filled with people like that, some even claiming to be Christian or Jewish, but living as if God doesn't exist, or doesn't count, if He does.

Hollywood's Jewish Factor

I think Bill could mount a very successful recruiting effort for the BMEA from Hollywood and New York media circles. Many of the candidates would be Jewish, since the industry is heavily populated by Jewish people. This isn't a wild assertion on my part, it's fact.

In 1988, Neal Gabler, a Jewish film historian, wrote, *Empire of Their Own: How Zukor, Laemmle, Fox, Mayer, Cohn and the Warner Brothers Invented Hollywood.* Gabler later changed the title to *An Empire of Their Own: How the Jews Invented Hollywood.*[2]

In 2010, columnist Joel Stein wrote:

> I have never been so upset by a poll in my life. Only 22 percent of Americans now believe 'the movie and television industries are pretty much run by Jews,' down from nearly 50 percent in 1964. The Anti-Defamation League, which released the poll results last month, sees in these numbers a victory against stereotyping. Actually, it just shows how dumb America has gotten. Jews totally run Hollywood . . ... The Jews are so dominant, I had to scour the trades to come up with six Gentiles in high positions at entertainment companies.[3]

Bill Maher is half Jewish by his own recognition. The son of an Irish father, he didn't know his mother was Jewish until his late teenage years.[4]

So, what is the link between the influence of Jewish people in media and the industry's general antipathy to the faith of Middle America? Judaism is the religion of the Jews, right? It's not that simple. Let me explain.

I sat at a dinner in a lovely home in small-town Pennsylvania with five churchgoing couples brought together by my host, the successful owner of a securities and investment firm. Because of my decades of work in the industry, the conversation turned naturally to questions and talk about Hollywood. The husband of one couple had had some experience in producing films and had well-formed opinions about a lot of things.

"Well, we all know the problem in Hollywood," the man boomed, "The place is run by Jews." I felt the hair beginning to bristle on the back of my neck and my blood pressure rising.

"Sir, that is not the problem." I was struggling to choose appropriate words.

"It is so run by Jews." He spoke as if none at the table had heard him the first time.

"I did not say that the leadership of the industry is not Jewish. I said that their being Jewish is not the problem. If anything, they are not Jewish enough. I wish they were more Jewish. They'd be more committed to the Torah and the teachings of the Hebrew Scriptures. The real problem in Hollywood is that the majority of leaders are *lost*. The "Jewish" are *lost*, the "Catholics" are *lost*, and a lot of nominal "Christians" are *lost*."

An awkward silence reigned around the dinner table before conversation picked up again.

"Lost" Is Not Just a TV Show

When I used this rather rare adjective in describing the culture in entertainment, I was using it in two distinct denotations—a *spiritual* definition and a *functional* one.

Being *spiritually lost* is, basically, not having found the path to spiritual peace, joy, love, forgiveness, salvation, inner power to overcome our baser nature, and hope beyond the grave. This is the definition which true followers of Jesus Christ use when they say they have been "saved." "Saved" is the opposite of "lost."

But, Hollywood is also *functionally lost*. Being functionally lost is *living by a set of guidelines that systematically dismantles your life*. Let me say that again: Being functionally lost is *living by a set of guidelines that systematically dismantles your life*. I believe most people in entertainment are functionally lost. For example, they truly believe that if they get rich, famous, powerful, and have lots of sex, they will be happy. Anybody want to join me in research into the lives of those who have achieved all of this? Want to discover the percentage who found living by these driving principles led them to inner peace, joy, and fulfillment? Want to study how many living out this philosophy ended up destroyed, bitter, alone, and in bondage to guilt, sexual deviancy, substances, or all three?

"Walk the Aisle . . . and Get Lost"

Those who walk the aisle at a Billy Maher Crusade end up lost, because he is an evangelist for lostness. But, he is not alone. There are Hollywood televangelists for lostness all over TV and in movies. They're just less in-your-face in their sermonic approach. Most of the lost in Hollywood are not embarrassed about being lost. They think being lost is cool, clever, enlightened, fashionable, and fulfilling. They think everybody should be lost. Many, like Billy Maher, preach lostness on TV, communicate the message of "lostianity" in movies, and hold their own version of public "crusades."

Don't get me wrong. Bill Maher isn't more lost than most of the rest. He's just more vocal and honest about his beliefs (or unbelief) and more passionate in recruiting others to his worldview. I like that about him. I refer to him and others like him who are very "out there" as "refreshingly lost"—no pretense. As Bill would say, "No B. S."

The "scary lost" are those who cloak their lostness in career-motivated charity work, involvement in politically correct causes, preaching empty platitudes about tolerance or acceptance of diversity, or, worse, flaunt their religiosity. This religiosity comes in many forms from superficial traditional religious practice to becoming part of the Cult of the Sweet Potato God (CSPG).

Don't laugh. As I write, there is probably a one-day CSPG seminar being planned for the ballroom at the Beverly Hilton or the Ritz Carlton in New York. Registration is a mere $5,000, and the hype will mention that "Hollywood's top people will be there." There will be testimonials from has-been actors who have found inner fulfillment—and weight loss—from a diet of sweet potatoes and wheat germ thanks to the spud deity. Attendees will be given "YAM IS GLAM" bumper stickers and a chance to have their picture taken with Brad and Angelina or some other "name" person from Celebrity for Hire, Inc. Scary lost. Is the CSPG an outlandish idea? You decide. I just saw an actual ad in Hollywood for Totemic Energy Jewelry!

Things Change as You Hit It Big

A frightening reality to Moral America is the incredible pressure the Hollywood culture exerts on those who enter the industry with a vibrant, innocent, devout faith—pressure to trash it and become like everybody else, lost.

The name Miley Cyrus comes to mind. When the Hanna Montana craze took off, Miley was a model of teenage virtue. She came to success from a family in which her dad, country singer Billy Ray Cyrus, had a reputation for holding his Christian faith dear. Miley had the hearts of the moms of America who allowed their daughters to watch her shows and buy gazillions of dollars of Hanna Montana stuff to imitate her. Her personal website in those years was right up front with the importance of her personal faith in Jesus Christ and the importance of God in her life.

Then, something happened. More than likely, a LOT of "somethings" happened. I don't know Miley's story, but let me piece together a likely scenario from the many other faith-focused young men and women I've watched hit it big and then jettison their faith and virtue.

Perhaps Miley started receiving messages—louder and louder messages—like:

- "You're growing up now, and this 'innocent child' thing isn't going to work now that you're thirteen/fifteen/a teenager."
- "You know, you've got to get more hip in what you wear. What's the harm in wearing some costumes that are little tighter/ shorter/skimpier/more revealing? You've got a nice body. Trust me, it will sell more albums, videos, and concert tickets."
- "Hey, we have a fun idea for a dance routine for your next show! We're going to have you dance around a pole and kind of slither up and down it. The scene will be very brief, but it will be hot." (This really happened.)
- "You know the Jesus thing you have on your website? Are you sure you want to lead with the religious stuff? Religion is a turn-

off for most people here, and there are a lot of people who are not Christians who will really resent your trying to proselytize them."

- "Hey, a wild idea for your performance on *Britain's Got Talent*. We've got a hot costume with ripped fishnet stockings, a skimpy basque, and you can pretend to do a lesbian kiss with another dancer. Whadaya think?" (This really happened.)

I don't know how Miley changed. I don't know who or what changed her. I'm not picking on her. All I know is that Hollywood changes people—especially people whose faith and virtue are paramount to them when they hit town.

The clincher to this argument came in February of 2011 when Miley's father, Billy Ray Cyrus, granted an interview with *GQ* magazine. In it, he said, "I'll tell you right now—the damn show destroyed my family . . . it's all sad." Asked if he wished the show had never happened, he said, "I hate to say it, but, yes, I do. Yeah. I'd take it back in a second . . .. For my family to be here and just be everybody okay, safe and sound and happy and normal, would have been fantastic. Heck, yeah. I'd erase it all in a second, if I could."[5]

Hebrew King Solomon observed in his wisdom writings that one of the things that make the earth tremble is "a servant who becomes a king" (Proverbs 30:21-22a). Hollywood makes royalty out of peasants, and they commonly don't know how to handle the privilege. So, the earth trembles.

KERCHUNK! KERCHUNK!

I toured the Ford automobile plant in Dearborn, Michigan, when I was a kid, and I still remember those giant steam presses that stamped a fender out of a sheet of rolled steel, KERCHUNK! The fender was kicked out, more steel fed in, and KERCHUNK! Hundreds of fenders identical to each other.

Hollywood is like those big presses using incredible pressure to form aspiring and wholesome young people into one more politically correct, faithless "fender" while pressing the God and Jesus stuff into scrap on the factory floor.

A beautiful, young, aspiring actress took a job as secretary for a friend of mine who headed a startup cable network. When I first met her, I noticed she had her Bible on her receptionist's desk. Commenting on it, I watched her glow and announce that she was, indeed, a believer in Jesus Christ, and that her faith was central to her life. She was hoping to come to Hollywood to make a difference. Not long after, she was different. The glow was gone as was the Bible on her desk. My friend who headed the company told me another exec had offered her two weeks with all expenses paid in London, if she'd sleep with him on the trip. She took the bait.

I've heard the rationalizations *ad nauseam* from the lips of these starry-eyed kids as they sell their souls one silly millimeter at a time:

"It's not the kind of work I'm proud of but . . .

- "I've been out of work for a year."
- "It'll look good on my resume."
- "I'll get to work with [Biggie]."
- "A lot of big people in this town started out doing work like this."
- "It should open doors to the kind of work I really want to do."
- "It'll pay the bills."
- "A person *has* to work!"

"I know I was stupid to sleep with him/her/them but . . .

- "I owe my break to him/her/them."
- "It didn't hurt to be seen with him/her/them."
- "I just couldn't say 'no' to [Mr. or Ms. Biggie]."
- "That's not the kind of person you say 'no' to out here."
- "I was afraid it could cost me a break if I didn't."
- "It was only once."

"It probably wasn't right to lie/steal/cheat/shift blame/destroy their reputation, but it was a break I just couldn't pass up."

On Sunset Boulevard, as in other places, souls aren't sold in one great auction. They are bartered away in thousands of tiny trades.

KERCHUNK! KERCHUNK! The giant Hollywood culture press strikes again, and the faith part becomes scrap.

Religious Bigotry . . . in "Tolerance Nation"?

My years of executive associations—and some very deep friend-ships—inside the entertainment industry have also uncovered some vicious anti-Christian attitudes and actions. A senior exec at a major studio told me that he left the studio when his Jewish superior made it clear that he would not get the executive position he was in line for and was *promised*, because he did not "fit in" with his Christian faith.

An angry Jewish TV network executive regularly mocked the faith of her personal assistant, a born again Christian. One day, the exec sneered and said, "Oh, are we wearing a big enough cross today? The Jew-girls coming for the meeting will certainly appreciate that."

I won't go into the vicious anti-Christian buzz around Hollywood before *The Passion of the Christ* was released. And this was before Mel Gibson's drunken anti-Jewish rants when arrested on Pacific Coast Highway.

Sharing Your Faith? You're Fired!

The anti-Christian bigotry comes from a broad spectrum of other of Hollywood's cultural icons, not just from secular Jewish people, to be sure. One of my first encounters with this vicious dynamic was in the early eighties.

My female associate met an incredibly competent woman execu-tive at Paramount Studios. I'll call her Shirley (not her name). Shirley held a co-executive position with a gay man who had lived with his lover for decades. He was a dark soul. Among other evidences of this darkness, he had a pantheon of demon figures on shelves in his office. Shirley said it was spooky even entering his office. There was an op-pressive spirit to the place.

Shirley needed her job. She was a single mom with two rising teen-agers and no other means of support. Because of this, she went the extra mile in her work. She attended performances on her own time looking for fresh talent, worked overtime, and had the recognition of her professional peers.

Shirley loved Jesus Christ. Her life was touched and made meaningful by her beliefs, and she faithfully tended them. Knowing that the place she worked was not a friendly environment for born again Christians, Shirley kept her faith close and quiet. She did find a couple of other women employees on the Paramount lot who were believers and, from time to time, would meet with them for lunch and prayer.

It was the time of year for her annual vacation. During the last week before her time off, her co-executive casually asked about her plans. Shirley said she was going to the East Coast, and indicated that she would be at Virginia Beach, Virginia, for a few days. When asked what was taking her there, she mentioned that she was making an appearance on a television show.

An Unwitting Mistake

"Oh, what show?" was the natural next question, and, not thinking, Shirley said, "It's called *The 700 Club*." The exec indicated that he had never heard of the show, and wished her a good vacation.

The interview with evangelist Pat Robertson on his *700 Club* show went well, Shirley thought. In the course of the conversation, she shared how she had come to faith in Christ, of the fellowship she had with a handful of Christian employees at Paramount, and how she had had the joy of introducing one female employee to faith in Christ. Nothing momentous, Shirley thought.

Shirley was wrong. When she got to back to Paramount the first day after her time off, she learned that she had been fired. Her office was cleaned out, and her personal effects were in boxes. Stunned and devastated, she probed for answers and got none. She did learn that the co-exec had viewed the interview or had reports of her Christian testimony on the show. Apparently, he was scandalized by the fact that she was "proselytizing" on the job and pressed for her termination. Shirley was out!

I was livid. I approached Shirley to discuss legal action against Paramount for wrongful dismissal or religious discrimination. After considerable prayer and thought, she decided not to pursue legal action. No small part of this decision was the fact that "This is a small town. If I sue, I may never get another job in Hollywood. Besides, I am trusting that God will take care of me." God did take care of her, but I was still enraged by the injustice.

We Don't Give a [Bleep]

I was on the Paramount lot to see another exec a short time later. Before I surrendered my pass at the gate, I asked security if I could use the Paramount "house phone." They consented, and I asked the operator to connect me to then studio head Michael Eisner's office. This was years before Eisner headed Disney/ABC.

When Eisner's assistant answered, I identified myself, indicated that Mr. Eisner was not expecting my call, and said I wanted to talk to him for just a couple of minutes. "I have some information which might save Paramount a lawsuit," I announced. There was a pause as I was put on hold, and then a man's voice identified himself as Michael Eisner.

"Mr. Eisner, I am not an attorney, and there is no threat involved in this call. But, I have been in management all my life, and sometimes things happen which—if we had only known about them—could have saved our companies a lot of grief. I am calling to tell you of such a situation involving a Paramount executive."

I had his interest. I went on. "A woman executive named [Shirley] in the [department] was just fired by [co-executive's name] because of her Christian faith. I am calling without her knowledge or approval, because I believe this is a case of wrongful dismissal or religious discrimination. I think you would be wise to look into it, and see if something can be done to rectify the situation."

"We don't give a [bleep] what religion people are around here. Why, Dan Curtis [producer, *Winds of War* miniseries and *Night Stalker* series] sits in his office with his Bible on his desk."

"I believe you, sir, but I believe you have some executives working for you who are not so tolerant. It's your decision, but I'd look into it. That's all." Eisner hung up without thanking me for calling. No surprise.

I found out from an attorney in the legal office of Paramount that they did look into it . . . and battened down the hatches. Of course, Shirley never sued, but being open about her Christian faith cost her dearly.

And, Then, There's Columbia

I called on a senior executive at Columbia Pictures in the eighties, a man I heard was a committed Christian. The very notion was a stunner, because that studio's bosses had a reputation for nixing all requests for Bible studies, prayer meetings or other religious meetings, and for being generally unfriendly to those of the Christian faith. I called on him, we became good friends, and he joined our Bible study and fellowship group which met in the conference room at CBS Television City.

One day, he left the lot to get lunch and heard a woman talking to a security guard at the gate. He thought he heard her talking about her faith. When he returned to the lot, she was still in the conversation, and he heard her mention prayer or praying.

"Excuse me, did I hear you talking about prayer?" The woman noted he was one of the executive "suits" and showed panic on her face. She thought she was in trouble, and meekly said, "Yesss."

"I am a Christian. If that's the kind of prayer you're into, let's talk. I've been thinking of starting a studio prayer meeting."

"Where would we meet?" the woman asked apprehensively.

"I can book the board room." The exec was confident.

Angst on her face, the woman asked, "What if they find out . . . and start firing people?"

"Of course, they'll find out. It's right across the hall from the head of the studio. But, if they start firing people, they'll have to start with one executive."

Relief flooded the woman's face, and that became the genesis of a studio prayer group which met every Wednesday for years in a conference room right near the studio chairman's office.

But why would any Hollywood professional have to ask, "What if they start firing people?" for holding quiet meetings to pursue their faith on non-company time? Who knows, the studio might have been able use some divine intervention on its behalf.

Dangerous People

Not only does Hollywood culture seem to have this visceral reaction to the faith of the conservative Christian and Jewish stripe, some indicate *fear* of them. On September 12, 2006, on ABC Television's *The View*, Rosie O'Donnell said:

O'DONNELL: "One second. Radical Christianity is just as threatening as radical Islam in a country like America, where we have a separation of church and state. We're a democracy."

UNIDENTIFIED FEMALE: "We are not bombing ourselves here in the country."

O'DONNELL: "But they [Christians?] are bombing innocent people and other countries, true or false?"

UNIDENTIFIED FEMALE: "But Christians are not threatening to kill us."[6]

In fairness, Rosie O'Donnell is not a spokesperson for Hollywood, but low-level suspicion and even contempt for conservative faith—if not fear—comes through Hollywood banter more often than one might expect. It's the kind of suspicion which is spread in propaganda when a society is mobilizing popular sentiment against a minority.

Bill Maher, leverage your celebrity status to hit the arenas and convention centers with your message, "Atheists of the world unite!" Hold your Billy Maher Crusades to mobilize the skeptics. You may gain a following, but I wouldn't bet on your ultimate success.

Furthermore, the Bill Mahers pose a far smaller threat than the "devoutly secular" with media influence who "live as if there is no God," and seek to silence those who love and serve Him.

CHAPTER SIX

A NOT-SO-DUCKY EPISODE

The Conflict over PC

Little did the 13,065 residents of West Monroe, Louisiana, realize that their sleepy little town would become the epicenter of an earthquake of "biblical proportions." Not even their 49,156 neighbors in Monroe could have imagined that one family across the Ouachita River in the other of the "Twin Cities of Northeast Louisiana" could have believed it could happen—62,221 beings shaken by tremors no one could have seen coming.

But the fuzzy-faced Robertson men with the pretty wives who were catapulted to global fame through the A&E channel's quasi-reality show *Duck Dynasty* were caught astride the shifting tectonic plates of the American media chasm. On one side of the crevasse, were Abbe Raven and Nancy Dubuc, bosses in the media power structure towering over the Robertson's show. On the other side, was *DD* family patriarch, Phil Robertson, and, of all things, the Bible! Unsuspecting people from West Monroe to Manhattan to Malibu were drawn to the two brinks of the divide.

The individuals who ended up toe-to-toe in the struggle could not have been more different. Abbe and Nancy are attractive and decent, if ambitious, female executives in a media world typified by the philosophical correctness (PC) of their professional peers.

This is a world I describe through the chapters of this book as living by three perceptions. The first is that the worldview they share with their New York and L. A. colleagues is absolute and inviolable (even though "absolutes" are strongly eschewed). The second perception is that their worldview is dominant in contemporary life in America. The third is that people who hold to a literal interpretation of the Bible and its clear definitions of "sin" are relics from some unenlightened era of human evolution.

The Robertsons—with their strange swamp-and-man-over-beast subculture—are different. They differ not only in their mud-, critter-, gun-, and hip-boot-filled surroundings, they differ in their basic perceptions of the nature of God, creation, abortion, homosexuality, morality, free enterprise, freedom, America, and much of the rest of life.

Clash. Bang. Boom.

It started when Phil Robertson granted an interview with *GQ* magazine, one in which he shared his unpolished beliefs on a wide range of topics. When the questions got to homosexuality, he did something almost never done in public discourse—he talked in his typically coarse, no-nonsense manner about what same sex couples DO with each other. He got beneath the sanitary it-doesn't-matter-who-you-love level of conversation to the behavior he can't understand and believes violates the Divine Writ of His God.

And he did so, not on the *Duck Dynasty* show—his comments would surely have been left on the cutting room floor—he did so for an outside print publication. That's when the refuse hit the whirling blades. Phil Robertson was immediately and indefinitely suspended from the show. Deeply offended by his Bible-based remarks, A&E execs rose above their cherished commitment to free speech and cast their lot with, in their own words, the gay and lesbian community,

> A&E said in a statement on Wednesday evening, 'His [Phil Robertson's] personal views in no way reflect those of A&E

Networks, who have always been strong supporters and cham-
pions of the GLBT community. The network has placed Phil
under hiatus from filming indefinitely."[1]

Running Against the Numbers

Quite against all business sense, the decision ran headlong into
some daunting numbers. Research by the Williams Institute at UCLA
based on four recent surveys sets the number of Americans who are
gay, lesbian, and bisexual at nearly nine million or 3.5% of the population—roughly the population of New Jersey.[2] Pit those numbers
against the 160 million who identify themselves as "Christian." Fold in
the millions of Muslims and Jews who share the biblical and Koranic
prohibitions against same sex behaviors in their religions. Add in the
millions of religiously agnostic who just don't like gay sexual practices.
The result? Frankly, not a fair fight.

Never mind that the decibel level of the 3.5% on this issue is radically higher than that of the rest of the populace. Set aside that the
widespread support the 3.5% have in entertainment, media, public
education, and some levels of government. There is an overwhelming
"silent majority" of people in America who view homosexual behavior
as either morally reprehensible, socially destructive, or personally not
to their taste.

But, candidly, Abbe and Nancy can't be faulted for not knowing
the odds against them. Their world has little association or rapport
with people of faith across the land. Their peers share their values and
worldview almost unanimously. In their world, the fight for GLBT rights
is the moral equivalent of the fight to end racial discrimination. In their
world, calling gay behavior "sin" or "deviant behavior" is "hate speech."
Funny that the vicious, vile, reprehensible attacks on Bible believers
coming from the GLBT community never draw the same label.

The Other Shoe Drops

So, how did the Phil Robertson episode play out? A&E execs got
a massive response, but not exactly what they expected. It was not a
national outpouring of support for their defense of the GLBTs. Instead,
it was a massive show of support for the Robertsons and their values

and—in the absence of that—a ringing endorsement of free speech and and religious freedom.

Two days before Christmas, an unnamed group launched a social media-based campaign to show support for patriarch Phil. Dubbed the National Chick-Phil-A Day, January 21 was promoted to show solidarity with him and, presumably, his moral positions. Supporters were advised to wear their *DD* gear and eat at a Chick-fil-A fast food restaurant." It could be said that the strange duck/chicken alliance comprised a sort of "fellowship of the fowl."

This was fitting since the Chick-fil-A chain was the object of protests by the GLBT community for comments made by its president, Dan Cathy, some time ago. At that time, Cathy spoke against gay unions and in support of the "biblical definition of marriage." His comments were not perceived well by the GLBT community and its sympathizers.

After both sides in the conflict generated more heat than light and the Robertsons and A&E had some intense interactions, the company caved. Phil Robertson was reinstated, the channel ran a *Duck Dynasty* "super marathon" on Christmas Day, the previously taped episodes including Phil will still air, and he will still be a feature on subsequent shows. The final score was Robertsons: 1, A&E: 0.

Jason Riley, editorial writer and board member of the Wall Street Journal, in an interview with Juan Williams on *The O'Reilly Factor* noted:

> [A&E] is acknowledging that it has massively misread the viewership of this program. I think there's a sense among A&E producers that people would tune into the show to mock or make fun of this family, but it turns out that people tune in because they share the values and sensibilities of these folks, and it's quite amazing how badly . . . A&E, with regard to its viewers, initially misjudged their customers.[3]

Cherchez La Bucks

Forgive the cynicism, but the outcome of this flapola was really pretty predictable. When it comes to show business, it is easy to forget that after all the glitz, glamour, hype, hysteria, and celebrity schtick, it is show **business**. The (financial) bottom line will remain the bottom line. When push comes to shove, no need to *cherche* for *la femme*. Search for the flow of moolah.

Look at it this way. A&E has a hit show going with ginormous ratings. It is a cultural phenomenon. It is also a lottery-winning-level corporate cash cow. The decision to shelve Phil Robertson threatened all of that.

Maybe A&E had never seen the bumper sticker in the Bible Belt that says, "The family that prays together stays together." But anybody who understands the family bonding of those who share a deep, commitment to Jesus would understand. Without being a fly on the wall in the meetings between the fuzzy faces and network execs, I can speculate with some certainty that the message was delivered clearly, "No dad, no deal."

There had to be at least a dozen other cable channels salivating like vultures to swoop in and pick up a successful ratings bonanza like *DD*, should the Robertsons find a way out of their A&E contract. The bosses at the channel had to know that.

In Hollywood, when the profit motive conflicts with lofty moral ideals, many, not all, media moguls will tend to "rise above principle." If there was ever a question about this, a 2013 bombshell book by Ben Urwand titled, *The Collaboration: Hollywood's Pact with Hitler* answered this question. Urwand's premise, clearly stated on his book jacket, is, "To continue doing business in Germany after Hitler's ascent to power, Hollywood studios agreed not to make films that attacked the Nazis or condemned Germany's persecution of Jews." Based on nine years of research, Urwand's prologue declares that "the studio heads, who were mostly immigrant Jews . . . followed the instructions of the German consul in Los Angeles."[4] The reason for this accommodation, if not collaboration, is clear to Urwand . . . and others. Germany was Hollywood's second largest source of box office revenue after the U.S.

Fake Bleeps

This was not the first run-in the channel bosses had with Robertson family values. Phil, Willie, Si, and the rest of the clan have some principles. Even if the show has some crude elements, the family's Christian faith comes through their prayers in Jesus' name, their basic virtue, their family love, and, yes, their language. The Robertsons learned that producers of their show felt the language needed a little spicing up as it is with *Pawn Stars, Rick's Restorations, Storage Wars,* and other reality shows with salty talk. So, the producers *edited bleeps into the show* even though there were no expletives behind them! When the Robertsons learned what was happening, they put a sure and sudden stop to the practice. They made it clear that they don't use that kind of language and didn't like creating the impression that they did.

When the family got flack "from Hollywood" for praying in Jesus' name, because it might offend, Phil Robertson countered, "What year is it?" Puzzled, the producers didn't know how to respond. Phil, told them, "It's 2012 *A.D.*, the year of our Lord, *Anno Domini.* If we count years from Jesus, we think that ought to be a good enough name to refer to from time to time." End of matter. Phil tells this story in a YouTube video.5

If you watch *Duck Dynasty*, what they say is what you'll get. You'll also hear the name of Jesus . . . not used as an expletive.

The Core of the Matter

At the center of the issue is one single hardcore antipathy. Hollywood will let you have any kind of religious notions you want. You can believe in the God of the Sweet Potato. You can believe in a god who is in you, with you, or that you are a god. You can espouse Eastern Mysticism, Scientology, The Course in Miracles, EST, or Buddhism.

All of this is AOK *unless* . . . your religious belief system has an objective definition of *sin* that includes behaviors in which the media populace engages! That kind of religion becomes an enemy of society. PC strikes again.

CHAPTER SEVEN

JESUS SAVES

The Conflict over Jesus and Being Born Again

Not Ready for Prime Time

It was an august setting. The annual conference of the National Association of Television Program Executives (NATPE) was, for decades, *the* trading market for television program content. Major studios, cable channels, TV networks, big station managers and programmers, and independent TV program producers had to be represented at NATPE to buy and sell programming. I have probably attended twenty-five of the shows in as many years.

NATPE has, for decades, been a big deal. In the show's heyday, one HBO exec told me that his company was going to spend $1 billion dollars at NATPE securing movies for the coming year. A Paramount exec told me the studio's budget for that year's NATPE convention was $11 million dollars. The Paramount exhibit was two or three stories high, food and beverage flowed freely, celebrity appearances were sprinkled throughout the schedule, and little rooms in the exhibit were abuzz with TV program dealmaking. It was much the same throughout the rest of the bustling exhibit hall and convention sessions.

As the industry has changed, NATPE has lost a lot of its drawing power and importance, but one event is still a feature—The Brandon Tartikoff Legacy Awards. The award is named for the widely respected former head of NBC programming who died of Hodgkin's disease at 48 years of age.[1] The Legacy Award was created "to recognize a select group of television professionals who exhibit extraordinary passion, leadership, independence, and vision [and who evoke] the spirit of Tartikoff's generosity."[2] It could well be called the "Legend Award," because honorees include the most successful people in the history of television.

At the 2009 convention, honorees included Tyler Perry, a one-man phenomenon filling huge arenas for his stage shows, securing unheard of contracts of his TV series like *Tyler Perry's House of Payne*, and *Meet the Browns*, and directing and starring in movies like *Diary of a Mad, Black Woman, Family Reunion*, and *Madea Goes to Jail*. In the award presentation, Tyler was credited with accomplishing more in his relatively short career than many have in their lifetimes.

In his acceptance speech to the top leaders in television, Tyler told how the executive at a big-three TV network told him he would have to take "Jesus" out of all of his shows, because Jesus just "didn't fit in prime time." Tyler, a committed Christian, refused to cave in to the executive's condition and turned down a lucrative network contract with the response, "I can't do that. I know my audience."

Misunderstanding the Audience

When it comes to the Faith Community, Hollywood doesn't "know its audience." Mastermedia International's Corporate Seminar, designed to demystify the evangelical community for media executives, has been wonderfully well received. Its reception is positive for one key reason—it opens their eyes to a huge, potential audience of up to 100 million people who spend $2.1 trillion dollars a year.[3]

Even larger than the 100 million who self-identify themselves as "evangelicals," there are millions more Americans for whom the Christian faith is a significant part of their lives. An additional 60 million claim the designation "Christian."[4] It would be pretty silly for any business to ignore a 160-million-person market!

This Christian worldview focus is lost on the creatives in Hollywood, many of whom apparently don't know any evangelicals or committed Christians well. They certainly don't know how they think when it comes to matters of faith. Projecting their secularism onto America, they actually edit out references to faith from their product.

A field producer for a major Los Angeles area TV station was sent out with a film crew to cover the story of a man who was living with and feeding homeless people. As the cameras rolled, the man was asked why this Good Samaritan was doing this—living in the open, giving his own money and time to these poor folks. He cheerily responded that his motivation was "the love of Jesus." He explained that he had been blessed by receiving Jesus' love and wanted to share it with others less fortunate than he.

Back at the station, the field producer—herself a devout follower of Jesus—checked on the edit of the footage and found out that the editor was doing his best to take out all the "Jesus stuff."

"You can't do that!" she said. "Without that element, the story makes no sense. It doesn't have to make any sense to us, but that *is* the story. The man says he is motivated by the love of Jesus."

Our team was holding a Corporate Seminar for executives from Time Inc. and making the point that it is unwise to edit out material treating faith. Our reason is this—given the highly religious nature of a huge segment of American viewers, more people will probably relate to the faith-focused content than the rest of the story.

The editor of a major national publication in the seminar told us the suggestion was relevant to a story her magazine was doing on *Everybody Loves Raymond* star Patricia Heaton. Patricia is very public about her beliefs. "We had a debate as to whether we were going to leave the part about her Christian faith in the article. In part because of your suggestion, we left it in. After all, we reasoned, that's who Patricia is."

Patricia Heaton Puts Things in Perspective

Patricia *is* outspoken about her faith. In an interview with Fox News anchor Bill O'Reilly in 2002, Bill asked about her being pro-life:[5]

O'REILLY: ". . . So you are pro-life in a town . . ."

HEATON: "That's right."

O'REILLY: ". . . that is almost 100 percent pro-choice. How does that impact on you?"

HEATON: "Well, you know, I'm a chairman of Feminists for Life, and so I think that, because of that, we have an interesting stand that most people don't—haven't heard before [sic], which is being pro-life can be a feminist issue." The early feminists were pro-life. And, really, abortion is a huge disservice to women, and it hasn't been presented that way. So—so it's a—there's a sort of an 'in' for me because of that take on it."

O'REILLY: "Do you take any heat from your peers out there?"

HEATON: "I did. I mean, I did originally. I vote Republican because of my pro-life stance, and, of course, that was a real hot-button issue when Bill Clinton was first elected. I mean, people really—I wore a Quayle-Bush button, and literally people would stop and look at the button then and look at me and give me dirty looks and, you know, say nasty things to me. I think, since 9/11, a lot of that has calmed down a little bit."

O'REILLY: "But, still, I mean, if Susan Sarandon or Barbra Streisand were here, I mean, they wouldn't talk to you. They would turn their back on you."

HEATON: "You know what? It's not that polarized. I mean, people know me first as an actress and friend."

O'REILLY: "But if they knew. If they knew, they. . ."

HEATON: "Some people have had that reaction, but I wouldn't say all of them . . . ."

"That Must Take Guts"

O'REILLY: "OK. Now that, obviously, takes guts in Hollywood because, in Hollywood, there's a subtext that, if you don't play the game, you know, you could lose jobs."

HEATON: "Yes."

O'REILLY: "Did you ever think of it?"

HEATON: "Yes, I've thought about it. On a personal level, as a Christian, it will not be Barbra Streisand I'm standing in front of when I have to make an accounting of my life."

O'REILLY: "Yes. You're not going to put your resumé up to . . ."

HEATON: "Yes, you know, so she . . ."

O'REILLY: "That's a good point."

HEATON: "She will not be in charge of, you know, whether I get my wings or not. So, ultimately, if I had to, I could pack all this up and do something else. There's three chapters in my book about all the survival jobs I've worked. I'm very happy to go back to that if I . . ."

O'REILLY: "So you—all right. So you're putting your moral—your moral beliefs . . ."

HEATON: "Life is very short."

O'REILLY: ". . . in front of your career."

HEATON: "Life is short. My mother died when I was 12. There's no guarantee that we're going to be here tomorrow."

Patricia Heaton's perspective is rare in Hollywood, where one's career is one's life. Typically, sacrificing a career for one's faith, especially in *Jesus*, is virtually unthinkable.

The Jesus Spin

Jesus is a popular subject around the world. He is the unique person of human history. Stories about Him get great readership. Movies and TV miniseries about Him tend to draw in the faithful—and the curious—in droves . . . despite Hollywood's conventional wisdom that "religion doesn't sell." *The Bible* miniseries on the *History* channel broke ratings records.

When Mel Gibson was shopping *The Passion of the Christ* around Hollywood, he had the door slammed in his face by a good number of studio gatekeepers and investors. I remember the buzz, "The film's a dog. It's going to be Mel's kooky Catholic take on the life of Jesus. It won't gross $20 million." The honchos wouldn't touch it, so Mel put tens of millions of his own money into its production and distribution.

I know a Christian studio exec who pleaded with the heads of his studio to, at least, sew up the video rights for the film. They wouldn't listen, until he said something like, "Look, secure the video rights. If it doesn't make money, fire me." The bosses relented. The DVDs of *The Passion of the Christ* reportedly grossed $20 million *the first month* for that studio![6] As you know, the theatrical release alone has now grossed nearly $612 million worldwide.[7] Estimates of its total take from all sources run as high as $1 billion.

Here is the rub. Execs know that, done right, Jesus sells. But, since they hate the subject, about the only motivation to do Jesus stuff is profit. And this is where they fall into a very deep trap. Knowing precious little about Jesus or His closest followers, they draw on counsel from those who are equally ignorant or skeptical about the subject. They end up putting lethal "spins" on the content that kill the financial success by turning devout viewers flat off.

The Jesus Bandwagon

After the incredible success of *The Passion of the Christ*, people asked me, "What's the response of Hollywood to the box office success of the movie?" I answered, "Anger . . . for a number of reasons. They are angry because it was Mel Gibson. He has a lot of people who don't like him. Anger because they don't like the subject matter. If the money had flowed to a film on almost any other subject, they would have liked it better. Anger because of sheer envy; they don't like it when others see this kind of incredible success. Finally, anger because they passed on the project and missed out on the gravy train."

So, *The Passion* makes gazillions of dollars and "Voilà!" Hollywood discovers the "religious market." The new mantra became, "There's gold in them thar' pews!" Studios started "faith" or "inspirational" divisions. Christian producers I know were getting meetings with people who wouldn't have touched them with a hundred-foot pole before. Everybody was looking for "The sequel to *The Passion*." I know of at least half a dozen scripts pitched using this line. Gatekeepers who have absolutely no appreciation for God—or certainly Jesus—got in line to "rise above principle," if there was money to be made. The head of one premium cable channel told me of *The Passion*, "I hated the movie. I just hated it. But, we'll probably run it. It'll get ratings." He ran it . . . twice. It got ratings.

It was really quite funny from the perspective of the Faith Community across America. All of a sudden, we believers had been "discovered" by Hollywood! We didn't even have to put on a slinky dress and hang around the Polo Room at the Beverly Hills Hotel. We were suddenly rising box office stars.

I've thought, what if it were a *knitting* movie that made hundreds of millions of dollars for its producers? Suddenly, studio execs would be scouring The American Association of Knitting Enthusiasts (AAKE—I made this up) for stories about knitting gauge, needles, blocking, and cable stitches. Studio research departments would be Googling the phrase, "Knit one, purl two." I can hear the pitch now, "It's Titanic meets Marian the Librarian. Marian takes a cruise with her knitting club. In heavy seas, Marion gets thrown overboard in shark-infested waters, but is saved by plunging her knitting needle into the heart of a Great White. It'll gross $200 million. Of course, we'll have to add a sexy scene to get a PG-13 rating. How about Marian lounging by the ship's pool in a hand-knit bikini?"

Absurdity Galore

The biggest vulnerabilities Hollywood writers and producers had after they "got religion" was (1) they knew precious little about Jesus and those who believe in Him, and (2) they didn't know what they didn't know.

You would have thought NBC would have learned after its fiasco with the expensive "biblical" miniseries, *Noah's Ark,* which bombed in 1999, because it was filled with ludicrous inaccuracies and anachronisms.[8] I remember the ratings were incredible until about thirty minutes into the first episode, then they tanked when it was clear to viewers that it made no sense whatever to anyone who knew the biblical story.

But NBC didn't learn. In 2005, the Peacock Network launched a second disaster supposedly for the Faith Community. A close friend and successful professional in Hollywood had occasion to be in a story meeting at NBC when execs were being pitched a TV series the creator was sure would tap this religious market.

- It had a religious title, *Book of Daniel.* The name would surely conjure up religious images among the faithful, both Jewish and Christian.
- Then, the lead character, Daniel Webster, would be an Episcopal priest. Fresh setting.
- Even Jesus would appear from time to time to the minister! Boffo!

The series was called "edgy," "challenging," and "courageous" in the NBC promotional hype.[9]

A few other story elements of the show I didn't mention:

- The minister is addicted to narcotic painkillers.
- His wife is fighting dependence on mid-day martinis.
- The 23-year-old son is homosexual.
- The 16-year-old daughter is arrested for drug possession in the pilot.
- The Reverend Daniel's brother-in-law absconds with church funds and abandons his family.
- A wimpy, white-skinned Jesus—who would have passed for a seventies hippie with a sort of "Whatever!" attitude—appears

to Rev. Webster and openly questions contemporary church teachings.

My friend, a devout believer, was incredulous. The execs were oohing and aahing and making comments about how fresh and creative the ideas were.

As the meeting was breaking up, my friend spoke up asking if the execs were open to another perspective. "I don't think this will work. I don't think viewers will be able to relate to the characters. Then, I think Christians will really be offended by the portrayal of Jesus. I don't think this series will make it to two episodes." The comments couldn't have been less welcome if he had added, "And you are all fifty pounds too fat."

Book of Daniel was a dog. NBC couldn't sell ads on the show. Eight affiliates refused to carry it. Several affiliates didn't air the second episode. It was canned after three.[10] So much for reaching the "religious market." NBC bosses didn't know what they didn't know. They don't get it.

"Jesus" Is a Four-Letter Word

It is common knowledge that in mainstream broadcast and cable television the "J-word" is more censored than the "F-word," unless, of course, "Jesus Christ" is used as an expletive. For its own reasons, the Hollywood gatekeepers don't want respectful treatment of Jesus or of conservative Christian belief. They'll cut it out any chance they get.

A very talented young writer and aspiring director moved to Hollywood about a decade ago to break into the business. Soon, his incredibly creative writing gifts were recognized, and he began selling some stories, some as TV "spec scripts" and some for feature films. He came from a devout Christian background in the Bible belt, was extremely committed to Jesus Christ, and kept himself chaste as a single man to honor his Lord.

I hadn't heard from him for a while when I received an email asking for some counsel. He had pitched a spec script for a Christmas movie to a major cable network, one he perceived most friendly to such faith-and-family-friendly fare. The network liked it and optioned it. As the script went through the approval channels at the network, it was presented for final edits to the top exec for the network on the West Coast.

My friend was stunned at the executive's comments, especially after he had already removed a Christmas Eve church service and a prayer at a football game for the same exec. Here are the comments verbatim.[11]

> Page 26 in Act 3—Is there another way to plant the raggedy man than through the father/St.Paul/ church scene? If [Name] Channel is the target for this project, religious content is off-brand for us (Emphasis added) . . ..
>
> Page 31 — The story of the dove and olive tree is a little religious and heavy-handed. Is there another symbol Barb could be knitting? Or if [writer's name] wants to use the dove/olive branch, can we trim out the religious back story and just leave it with the dove of peace?
>
> Page 68 — I think the nativity suggestion sounds religious. It's enough that he asks Marie what she would like built in her park. (Remember, this is a Christmas special!)
>
> Page 71 — It sounds less religious if she wants to go see Westminster Abbey instead of pray there. Also, isn't the attraction here that most of the kings and queens of England are buried at Westminster? (This wish is from a dying woman who wants to travel before she dies.)
>
> Page 75 — The mailman praying for Cyrus's wife and son sounds too religious. I think it's enough that he asks how they're doing.
>
> Last note — I don't think the title is Christmassy or enticing enough.

My friend's response was telling . . . and admirable.

> So take a look . . .. I'm disturbed by the seeming agenda to neuter God from a CHRISTMAS movie by [Network Name] of all places, a company that's been behind some sterling produc-

tions with religious content. Kind of ironic that they asked for a more "Christmassy" title, but want to delete any allusions to God or religion at all . . ..

For me, this is a situation akin to "eating the King's meat." I need to work, but it's not worth starving my soul or my integrity before God.

My friend didn't know that the head of the network was a friend and a man of faith. After some interaction with him in which I shared the writer's story and the executive's notes, things changed. The writer was asked to resubmit the script. This was an exception. Usually, Movie City secularists prevail in expunging the Jesus and Christian stuff.

Denial Is a Helpful Ally

Over the last three decades, it is stunning how many people in the media have come to have what evangelicals call a "born again" experience. When it does happen, it makes those around them extremely uncomfortable.

Years ago, a Jewish producer had an experience meeting a born again Christian couple at a Malibu party of industry people. At that point in his life, the producer was desperate. He had lost his marriage and family because of his philandering, was doing drugs as a coping strategy, and seeking spiritual help from a psychic and a palm reader. He had smoked a number of joints of marijuana on the way to the party and, for some unknown reason, was getting no "buzz" from the joints.

He was drawn to the Christian couple, whom he had never seen before, because "they glowed." In conversation, the two represented that it was their faith in Jesus that gave them this spiritual light.

Skipping out on his plans to party with a friend and some available women, the producer went straight home. On the balcony of his plush Malibu home, he was struck with chest pains and thought he was having a heart attack. Then, it happened. He says he heard an audible voice of comfort and of hope. At the Christian's office the next morning, he told of the incredible voice and its assurances, then asked, "I wonder if that was Jesus Christ?" It was. He burst into tears and surrendered his life to Jesus on the spot.

The radical change in his life became evident to all and was an embarrassment to many. He told me, "When I was destroying my family, sleeping around, doing drugs, and seeking help from psychics and palm readers, nobody told me I was crazy. When I told them I had discovered a new life in Jesus Christ, they said, 'You're crazy!'."

It is common for those in the Hollywood culture to rationalize, explain away, deny, or even mock and ridicule the dramatic changes in the lives of those who have a born again experience.

"Keep Away from My Granddaughter!"

I have an Oscar-winning friend who is a devout believer. He told me of one evening when he was called out of bed late at night by a young woman who was in a Bible study he held in his home in Beverly Hills. She was desperate. Her friend had overdosed on drugs, was in the hospital, and might not live through the night. She begged my friend to get out of bed and come to the hospital to share his faith with the drug abuser.

Reluctantly, he did so. He went to the hospital bedside of this young adult woman and found her lucid. He offered divine help through the supernatural power of Jesus Christ, if she would open her life to Him. She did so in prayer.

In the months that followed, the young woman was delivered from drugs, became part of his Bible study group, and became an enthusiastic witness to the change in life she had experienced. In getting to know her, my friend discovered that the woman was the granddaughter of one of Hollywood's most powerful execs . . . whom he knew.

Then, it happened. The exec called him into his office, tried to seduce him with job offers, and then railed on him to keep away from his granddaughter. He accused my friend of drawing her into a religious "cult." My friend protested that the young woman was an adult, capable of making her own decisions, and that his Bible study was no cult. Then, he threw down the challenge: "Do you like the changes you see in your granddaughter? Is she not clean from drugs and getting her life in order?" The exec had to admit that this was the case, but—true to form—denied that her newfound faith had anything to do with it.

Today, the biggest story like this is that of notorious Hollywood bad-boy writer Joe Eszterhas. After building a reputation for both sleazy movie content from *Basic Instinct* to *Showgirls* and a debauched lifestyle, Joe met Jesus Christ. He has written the story of his life transformation in a book called *Cross Bearer*. More about Joe later. The Hollywood cultural arbiters are already marginalizing or denying the validity of Joe's experience.

It's not cool to be born again or "get religion," as it is more often described. It is suggested that such an experience probably doesn't even happen. But I have a data base of more than 4000 media professionals who would stake their sacred honor on the fact that the experience is real . . . and life changing . . . because they've experienced it. More about this later, too.

Fox News' Secret Weapon?

If there is any phenomenon that is galling to many in film and television, it is the meteoric rise and incredible ratings (and financial success) of Fox News Channel (FNC). In a recent episode of cable's most-watched news show, *The O'Reilly Factor*, it was revealed that the Fox News Channel has ALL twelve of the top-rated cable TV news shows! MSNBC was 28th. Fox News typically more than doubles the ratings of its nearest competitor, MSNBC, and has more viewers than all the rest of the cable news channels combined . . . including CNN.[12]

While interacting with CNN executives, I talked to two execs who told me they had been hired to get CNN's ratings up to those of Fox. They said that as they began to analyze the demographics of FNC's viewership, they discovered that "Fox *owns* the evangelicals of America." By this, they meant that evangelicals and other conservative Christian viewers watch FNC in extremely large numbers and are loyal to it.

What is the secret weapon Fox deploys that has catapulted the channel to the top for more than a decade? I have an idea. I believe that, in large measure, it is because the channel is "faith friendly." Since its inception, the channel has been particularly open to the inclusion of content that is an expression of personal faith.

Roger Ailes, FNC President, says it succinctly, "I, and Fox News Channel, respect <u>all</u> religions, including Christianity, and denigrate no one. Some networks do not treat Christianity fairly."[13]

Without question, the American Faith Community, including Christians, feels comfortable with Fox. The Fox mantra, "Fair and Balanced," surely prevails in treating matters of faith, if for no other reason than it doesn't censor them out! In mainstream news, religion is typically not treated at all, unless the news falls under one of two categories—ceremonies and scandals. You might get mention of a Christmas mass at the Vatican or a Rosh Hoshana celebration. You surely will get coverage of a pedophile priest or a lecherous televangelist.

Viewers can clearly see the contrast to other TV news outlets. A viewer can watch Fox News and actually see on-air hosts wearing symbols of their faith, referencing their belief in God or even in Jesus Christ, and treating references to church and prayer and the Bible positively. This same fair treatment is shown to those of non-Christian faiths.

If demographic analysis shows that Fox "owns" the 100 million evangelicals—and many more of the nearly 200 million people who share traditional Judeo-Christian values—this factor may well be a key to FNC's success.

As they say in the TV business, "That's a lot of eyeballs."

CHAPTER EIGHT

"DEATH TO CONSERVATISM!"

The Conflict over Moral and Political Liberalism

Part I: *Moral* Liberalism

Is Hollywood Really the "Left" Coast?

"Secret meetings." "Speaking in whispers." "Hiding one's true religious and political beliefs to avoid being blacklisted and losing work." Are these expressions describing Christians in the underground church in the Peoples Republic of China? No, they are descriptions of the experience of moral conservatives in Hollywood.

Screenwriter and author Andrew Klavan (*Brooklyn to Manhattan, One Missed Call, Shock to the System*), speaking to a conservative journalist, said, "There is a culture in Hollywood where, if you are a left-winger, you can speak very openly—even in business meetings. If you are a conservative, especially a religious person, people have to meet in secret. They talk in whispers. It's a very disturbing kind of culture."[1]

Klavan shared the experience of Academy Award-winning actor Denzel Washington in making the movie, *The Book of Eli*, which is about a post-apocalyptic world in which the hero's mission is to protect the last remaining copy of the Bible. "The studio kept coming to him and saying, 'Could you cut out some of the references to the Bible? Could you cut out some of the religious references?'"

It is not uncommon for political conservatives in Hollywood to describe the isolation and rejection they experience if their peers get wind that they are Republican or conservative or deeply committed to Jesus Christ. Likewise, those who are part of the conservative political movement in America often make the charge that Hollywood and the entertainment industry are dominated and controlled by those "from the left" or "the liberals."

There is considerable research data to turn this assertion into fact. Research by the Pew Research Center's Project for Excellence in Journalism surveyed 222 journalists and news executives at national outlets. Only six percent considered themselves politically "conservative" and two percent "very conservative." In the general population 36 percent consider themselves conservative. Four times that number claimed tags "liberal" or "very liberal."[2]

In analyzing the conflict between the values of Hollywood and those of Middle America, let me focus at this point on *moral* liberalism rather than *political* liberalism. Of course, there is an overlay, but moral values run deeper than political affiliations. Furthermore, there are some moral liberals and moral conservatives in both political parties.

Definitions

A *moral conservative* is one who has an objective definition of morality that derives from divine revelation—be that the Torah, the Old Testament, or the New Testament. This morality is not alterable to accommodate shifting circumstances, perceptions, or feelings. It is constant and virtually nonnegotiable.

A *moral liberal* is one who has no objective definition of morality that derives from God's revelation. Typically rooted in some form of humanism, the moral liberal's value system is based more or less on rationalism, subjective criteria, intuition, or feelings. It tends to be variable and relative, since it is not based on absolutes.

I must credit Jewish author and talk show host Dennis Prager for introducing me to this analysis of moral liberalism and conservatism through a talk he gave a number of years ago.[3]

The Significance of Inanimate Objects

Liberals find problems and solutions in inanimate objects rather than in human character. For example, in dealing with the threat of nuclear war, moral liberals propose that we ban *bombs*. This approach ignores the fact that the U.S. has more nuclear weapons than any other nation, yet hasn't used them on anybody since 1945. Then, they were used on a despotic regime which threatened to destroy and enslave much of the world. Iran and North Korea have few nukes, if any, and are arguably more of a terror to the planet than the U.S.

Sexually transmitted diseases and teen pregnancy are approached with *condom* distribution rather than abstinence. The absence of free condoms doesn't impress morally conservative people as the cause of this problem.

Street violence is viewed as an issue of controlling *guns* rather than building moral responsibility in using firearms—giving rise to the moral conservative's bumper sticker, "Guns don't kill people. People kill people." Never mind that the State of Israel has higher per capita gun ownership than any other nation on earth, yet there is no terror on the streets of Jerusalem in the wee hours of the morning.

Then, ineffective education is caused by insufficient *money* for the system. The cure is to increase school funding, rather than placing people with more virtue into schools and ridding the system of those with incompetence and flawed character.

Ironically, the cure for drug addiction, smuggling, and the drug wars proffered by moral liberals is legalization of the inanimate substance. An approach which bans bombs and guns and legalizes drugs? Isn't there a disconnect here somewhere?

Bombs, guns, condoms, funding—sound like the issues you see championed by Hollywood celebrities? Not so in Flyover U.S.A. Bombs and guns are fine in the hands of those with virtue. Exercising sexual restraint is a better answer to teen pregnancy and STDs than free condom distribution. High-character educators always trump government programs and subsidies in improving schools. And because drug abuse, gambling, and prostitution are not inanimate objects but *enslaving behaviors*—which feed on man's baser nature and multiply social pathologies—they need to be prohibited by law.

The Double-Edged Approach to Institutions

One of the strange anomalies of moral leftists is their approach to institutions. On one hand, they are enemies of private corporate institutions like big business, Wall Street financial giants, Walmart, and big oil. Despite this visceral contempt for the aforementioned, they place confidence in big government institutions. Cases in point: poverty is to be cured by big government welfare—not work for the able, private charity for the unable, and loving intra-family support for both.

Racism and abuse are to be addressed by big government re-education, court-ordered "affirmative action," racial quotas, rehabilitation programs, and legislation against "hate crimes." Absent are emphases on spiritual repentance and divine redemption. Moral liberals typically don't recognize any solutions involving the human spirit. In fact, socializing the populace into spiritual virtues like the Ten Commandments is taboo. The Decalogue must be ripped down from public walls. How many Hollywood types have you seen championing government intervention to stop child or spousal abuse vs. those proposing a call for national repentance and spiritual renewal to eradicate same?

While moral liberals seek big government institutional control and intervention to solve social pathologies, they are rarely in support of institutional law enforcement or the military. Police and those in military service are often lampooned in movies and TV shows as dumb, corrupt, power-hungry, bloodthirsty, or dangerous.

This perspective nudges moral liberals to condemn warfare and police brutality. Because a common view in the leftist community is that mankind is essentially good—as opposed to moral conservatives' view of flawed humanity—the weapons and bombs of soldiers and the guns and nightsticks of the police are, at best, unnecessary and, at worst, "immoral." In the seventies, vets returning from Vietnam were abused and attacked as "murderers" and "baby-killers," and police were designated "pigs" by the counterculture. This antipolice sentiment gave rise to the bumper sticker, "If you hate police, next time you are in trouble, call a hippie."

Three Mistakes

A major error, here, is the denial of a basic human verity: Some evildoers (a term uncommon in liberal taxonomy) are so violently aggressive that only the use of force is capable of restraining them. Ever hear of Nazi Germany, Imperial Japan, or Al Qaeda?

Three mistakes underlie these differences. Foundational to nearly all of these differences between the two worlds of liberals and conservatives is the belief in, or failure to believe in, the existence of the eternal human soul. It is difficult to exaggerate the implications of this one issue in the great divide.

The belief that every human is, at the core, a spiritual being possessing a divinely bestowed, eternally existent soul is the game changer. In this "soul package" comes intrinsic worth, transcendent moral capacity for good and evil, and moral accountability to the One Who created and bestowed the soul. Absent this, a human is a collection of atomic particles assembled and manipulated by chance factors over time and possessing no more value or transcendence than a dish rag. Thus, with (1) no divinely established plan or rules for thought or behavior, (2) no future or judgment beyond the grave, and (3) no need for or hope for redemption, the race is left to grab all the sensate gusto, ego-fulfillment, and personal advantage possible. Period. "Morality" and "virtue" be damned; they are non-issues. Failure to believe in the existence of the transcendent soul of every person is mistake number one, and it underlies all the rest of the mistakes.

A second mistake is the lack of focus on character—personal, moral responsibility. Institutions—private or public—run by humans *without virtue* are exponentially more destructive and oppressive than the problems they were created to solve. This is the story of corporate robber barons and despotic governments throughout history. As someone has said, "A government big enough to meet all your needs is powerful enough to suppress all your freedoms."

A third mistake of this approach is ignoring divine *favor* and *judgment* on nations. Moral liberals dismiss out of hand the notion that, somehow, God's blessing and favor on a nation and its people is pivotal. They'll say boldly that God has nothing to do with all this . . . accompanied by Frank Sinatra singing, "I did it my way." The very religious Moral Center of America believes that God exalts and brings down nations based on the core of faith and righteousness of the populace. The irreligious mock the "God and country" people and their passion for this emphasis.

The Feelings Culture

I hosted a TV talk show in the late seventies, and one of the guests was a psychologist and a moral liberal. The subject was teen sex and pregnancy. When a member of the audience suggested that a solution might be saving sexual involvement for the covenant bond of marriage, the psychologist erupted, "But teenagers *can't ignore their feelings!*"

Moral America doesn't buy that. If we have feelings that we'd like to lynch our spouses or teenagers or bosses, we are expected to restrain those impulses. If our sex drives kick in while in the presence of another person's spouse, we know that those feelings have to be suppressed. If we feel like screaming at lazy or abusive bureaucrats during an IRS audit, for example, we usually find ways to restrain those feelings.

I once interviewed on stage a cherubic octogenarian couple to honor them on their fiftieth wedding anniversary. I asked them, "Have you ever considered divorce?" The wife, with a twinkle in her eye, said, "Divorce, never! Murder, definitely." Obviously, she had to suppress those murderous feelings. It's what all morally responsible people do.

The feelings culture, however, gives much more weight to feelings and sentiment. When those on the moral right use the phrase "bleeding-heart liberals," they typically are referring to moral liberals who are willing to set aside, law, policy, fair play, justice, and equal treatment to provide for special groups or individuals they view as "victims."

Victimology

This rather common Hollywood viewpoint was expressed in an incident in which Paris Hilton faced a judge for one of her numerous violations of the law involving drugs, resisting arrest, etc. She pled guilty. After the judge had reprimanded her and sentenced her for her offenses, her friend said of the judge, "He was soooo mean!"[4] Likewise, for moral liberals, it is *mean* to expect women to bring unwanted pregnancies to term, *mean* to demand that people who break into our country illegally face deportation, or *mean* to expect serial killers to give their life for those they have taken. Accepting full moral responsibility and taking justly due punishment for misbehavior, admittedly, doesn't feel good. It's just *right,* and it often ignores the pain of others truly victimized by evil behavior.

For moral conservatives, successful living is a matter of *virtue* such as faith, perseverance, industry, integrity, purity, loyalty, confession, forgiveness, etc. These are not attributes commonly praised among the moral left.

Moral conservatives abhor promiscuity, homosexuality, and adultery not just because they violate a Higher Law, but because they don't *work*! If these practices were good and true, everyone would be enriched and fulfilled by engaging in them! As it is, promiscuity destroys our ability to give and receive true love. Homosexuality is so spiritually debilitating that it reduces one to the point of depression and suicide—as indicated by the suicide rate among gays. Adultery "reduces a person to a loaf of bread" (a proverb from the Hebrew Scriptures) through rejection, betrayal, heartache, economic disaster, scarred lives of children involved, and destructively complicated life circumstances.

Pushing the Envelope . . . the Other Direction

In thirty-some years in Hollywood, I have never ceased to marvel at the pride taken by Hollywood writers, producers, and directors in "being edgy" and "pushing the envelope" in their media content. The marvel is that the edge being broached and the envelope getting pushed is always in the direction of more explicit, dark, destructive, and perverse content. It's commonly directed to defying traditional or conservative moral limits. Just once, I'd like to hear the Movieland creative establishment exult in their going "closer to the edge" of pure virtue and "pushing the envelope" toward more uplifting, righteous, inspirational, positive, and morally enriching content.

It hasn't happened yet, except among a handful of folks who, clearly, are moral conservatives—people who often have to keep their faith and virtue under wraps to be employable.

Part II: *Political* Liberalism

The Same Bird

One of my friends, before he went to his reward, was Dr. E. V. Hill, pastor of Mount Zion Missionary Baptist Church in Los Angeles. He and I built a training center in South Central L.A. for young people about to embark on international service with a kind of Christian Peace Corps. Students at the center lived with African American families and served under the supervision of about a dozen South Central church pastors, none of whom were white, though nearly all the students were.

I loved Pastor Hill. He was a big man with a bigger heart and an infectious ability to inspire and motivate people. In twenty minutes of speaking, he'd have you laughing and crying and ready to take on the world.

E. V. had no little political clout in Los Angeles. His church was huge, and he spoke for African American (he refused to use any term but "black") people—and the depressed South Central L. A. area—before, during, and after the neighborhood was torn apart by the awful Watts riots of 1965. I heard him say once, "We black folks have had experience with the *right* wing, and we have had experience with the *left* wing. And we have found that both of them wings is off the *same bird!*"

A-List Conservative-Bashers

If there is any assurance you can have about Hollywood, it is that the place is dominated by the *political* left. This is a real sticking point for political conservatives and one reason, of many, those from the Red States dislike Hollywood. I have very conservative Republican friends who are still ticked off at actor Alec Baldwin and director Robert Altman for not fulfilling their pledges to leave the country if George W. Bush got elected.[5] Baldwin reportedly got buried with demands that he head across the border after the election results confirmed Bush as President, demands probably coming from Flyover Country.

The visceral contempt and disrespectful language of mainstream Hollywood for "W" was unparalleled in my memory. "Hate" is not too strong a word to use. William Keck, writing for USA Today provided some frightening examples.[6] At a Kerry Fundraiser in 2004, Whoopie Goldberg made several crude, sexually-referenced puns on the President's last name. Ozzy Osbourne sang "War Pigs" while projecting a photo of protesters with images of Hitler and Bush in juxtaposition. Hip hop artist Jadakiss' hit "Why?" blamed Bush for the 9/11 attack on the Trade Center. From the Smothers Brothers to Donald Sutherland to Jane Fonda to Ed Asner to Martin Sheen, Hollywood has had a large-and-continuing contingent of A-list folks who have expressed contempt for political conservatives and aggressively sought to persuade America to liberal viewpoints.

If one tries to think of politically conservative celebrities bold enough to stand for their beliefs, the list is pretty short. Names like Charlton Heston, Pat Boone, Patricia Heaton, and Jon Voight come to mind. The reason is clear. When Jon Voight went on Fox News Scarborough Country and shared his conservative political perspectives, writer Noel Sheppard, writing for NewsBusters, suggested that some of his comments were ". . . likely to get him tossed out of Club Hollywood, if he's not careful."[7]

Attacks on conservatives are not limited to celebrity comments on talk shows or to the press or to marginalizing conservatives in Hollywood. They are also embodied in wildly irresponsible and bi-ased productions like Michael Moore's Bush-bashing documentary, Fahrenheit 9/11. It purports to examine America in the aftermath of the September 11, 2001 attacks, particularly the record of the Bush administration. Stunningly, it alleges links between the families of George W. Bush and Osama bin Laden, suggesting some kind of implication of President Bush in the World Trade Center attacks.

Moore's attempt to serve liberal political causes with the film was clear. "He announced that Fahrenheit 9/11 would not be in consideration for the 2005 Academy Award for Best Documentary Feature, but instead for the Academy Award for Best Picture. He stated he wanted the movie to be seen by a few million more people, preferably on television, by election day."[8]

The Liberals' Apocalyptic Nightmare

In 1990, I had an incredible experience. After the trauma to the Christian community—and to me personally—by the 1988 release of *The Last Temptation of Christ* by Universal Studios, my expectations of fair treatment from industry execs were, frankly, pretty low.

It was at this time that Bioscop Film and Cinecom Entertainment Group et. al., released *The Handmaid's Tale*. The buzz on the movie reached the Christian community from some critics who had screened the film, and it smelled like it could be *The Last Temptation of Christ* scene all over again. Reports were that it was a real hit job on Christians.

On its face, the production had some real credibility. Its list of stars was impressive—Natasha Richardson, Faye Dunaway, Aidan Quinn, Elizabeth McGovern, Victoria Tennant, and Robert Duvall, for starters. Impressive.

The story was based on a speculative novel by Canadian author, Margaret Atwood, and portrayed a moral and political liberals' worst nightmare. In a post-nuclear-war futuristic setting, the U.S. is taken over by an oligarchy of militaristic fundamentalist Christians. Because of the effects of radiation on fertility, women who can bear children are extremely scarce. Thus, the oligarchs use their totalitarian power to impress all fertile women into the equivalent of fundamentalist convents. There, they are trained by ruthless female equivalents of Catholic "mother superiors" to become servile to the national leaders for their sexual use and procreation. The "handmaids" are also indoctrinated into conservative Christian culture through religious ceremonies. The top government boss, the Commander, is played by Robert Duvall, and the tag line on the film was, "A haunting tale of sexuality in a country gone wrong."[9]

Not difficult to see where this is going. In one scene, characters played by Duvall and Dunaway are having sex while a TV in the room shows Dunaway's character in a church service. She is singing

"Amazing Grace." "Amazing grace, how sweet the sound that saved a wretch like me. I once was lost, but now am found, was blind but now I see."

Think about it. Here was America's favorite Christian hymn—one deeply revered by believers everywhere—juxtaposed with a sex act by the corrupt "commander" of a right wing "Christian" tyranny. This was as vicious a portrayal of cynical contempt for conservative Christian faith as one can imagine.

Aren't You Going to Protest?

Right before the film was to hit the theaters, I got a call from a young lady saying she was with a film distribution company. I took the call and, the way I remember it, the conversation went something like this:

"Dr. Poland, I am with [film distribution company], and I understand that you were involved in the protest against The Last Temptation of Christ. Is that true?"

"Yes, I got drawn into it."

"Well, our company is distributing a new release called The Handmaid's Tale. Have you heard of it?"

"I have. It sounds like it may well portray Christians in a very unfavorable light."

"In light of that perception, I'm wondering if the Christian community is planning to protest the film."

"No."

There was a long silence, and then the caller said, "May I ask why not?"

"Sure. To attack Jesus is blasphemy. To attack Christians is often justified."

This silence on the other end of the phone line was even longer. It was as if the woman was disappointed that no protest was planned, and she didn't know how to respond.

Then, I think I surprised her even more. "Would there be a chance I could talk to the head of your distribution company?" She offered to put me through, and a man with a Jewish surname picked up.

"May I help you?"

"Yes, one of your representatives just called me to see if the Christian community was planning to protest the showing of *The Handmaid's Tale*, and I wanted to get more of your perspective."

"Happy to provide it."

"Sir, generally speaking, would you feel comfortable distributing a film that demeaned a racial, ethnic, or religious group?"

"No."

"Well, I haven't seen this film, but the reports of those who have say that it is a very vicious attack on those of the Christian faith. As a member of that community, I wondered what your position was."

"I haven't really perceived it as that, but, no, I wouldn't support a film I thought was an unfair treatment of any religious community."

"That is very gratifying to hear. Like I said, I haven't seen the film, so maybe the reports are not accurate, but I thought I'd ask."

"Let me tell you what I'll do. The film's now showing in a theater in Beverly Hills. I'll have a courier deliver two tickets to a showing there. Take a friend, view the film, then get back to me with your comments. I'd like to hear them after you've seen the film."

We made arrangements for the delivery of the tickets, I thanked him, and I hung up the phone dazzled at the gracious and reasonable response I received from this man I'd never met.

Awful.

There is probably no other word to describe this R-rated product than "awful." I took a film producer friend of mine, and we sat through a flick that had precious little to recommend it from any perspective. Its hypothetical portrayal of the baseness and debauchery of a tyrannical government would have been bad enough. But for the story line to postulate that this government was ruled by men whose debauchery and oppression flowed out of or through their faith in Jesus Christ was outrageous.

The notes my producer friend and I took by tiny flashlight in the theater were put into readable form, then I called the head of the distribution company to chat about the content. Once again, he was extremely gracious and reasonable. He listened patiently, seemed to understand some of our objections to the content, and then responded. "Dr. Poland, you really don't have to worry about this film. It isn't going anywhere. It's not doing well at the box office, and if you let it, it will soon die a natural death."

After the spectacularly fair and decent treatment from the head of the distribution company, I thanked him profusely for his kindness, for arranging for the tickets, and for listening to my concerns. I invited him to lunch on my next trip to his city.

He thanked me with equal profusion, saying that he had had some calls from Christians that were, to say the least, not gracious nor reasonable. He mentioned the name of a prominent Christian film critic in Hollywood. He accepted my invitation to a future lunch.

Die, the movie did. It made it into only 177 theaters and grossed less than $5 million.[10] While I don't know the film's production costs, just considering its high-priced cast, somebody lost a lot of money. More important, *The Handmaid's Tale* didn't get its slanderous message against conservative Christians to the masses.

Sometime later, the film distributor and I met for lunch. We have become extremely close friends in the two decades since. We have shared deep affection and interaction over his Jewish faith and mine in Jesus.

Maybe bridges *can* be built across this great divide between Hollywood and the Faith Community. It just might happen if we set aside labels like "Christian" and "Jewish" and "conservative" and "liberal" and sit down together in good faith and talk . . . and, more important, listen.

Just maybe.

CHAPTER NINE

THE HEF AND PARIS FACTOR

The Conflict over Excess

It was a story meeting with famed film director Steven Spielberg. A producer friend of mine was in the meeting as Steven described a character in the story line. He painted the guy as a kind of "American Everyman"—married, wife and two kids, goes to work every day, lives in a $500,000 house . . .. Whoa, what did you say? He ". . . lives in a $500,000 house . . .."? My friend said, "Steven, the typical American doesn't live in a $500,000 house."

My friend was right. The median price of a *new* home about the time Steven made this observation was probably under $200,000.[1] The price for a previously owned home in the Midwest and South where most Flyovers—most of the "Everyman" and "Everywoman" people live—would have been closer to $125,000. It's about $150,000 today, many years later.[2]

I'm not faulting Steven Spielberg, but the comment may have reflected the very different world in which Hollywood and New York media professionals live and work from that of America's Everyman. Many of the media elite live in a world of comparative excess.

A half a million dollars doesn't buy much house in Malibu or Manhattan, or for that matter, in many of the 'burbs of those two areas. I considered moving closer to Hollywood a few years ago, and faced two realities. One, my wife and I would have to downsize from the $315,000 home we currently occupy. Two, I would have to get paid about $300,000 a year to cover the mortgage on our downsized home, a multiple of what I get paid now!

Those numbers are staggering to people in the "I" States where the median annual income per family—many with two wage earners—was $49,777 in 2009, and not much more in recessionary 2010.[3] Middle America sees the media world as a world of excess in many dimensions, not just income and cost of housing.

Limo, Please

New Orleans is a convention city. The Ernest N. Morial Convention Center is the nation's sixth largest, and downtown hotels host events of 100,000 or more. Attending the annual convention of the National Association of Television Program Executives (NATPE) a number of years ago, I struck up a conversation with an old friend. I met him when he was head of programming at channel 11 in Los Angeles in the early eighties. He later left and joined a convention management company that contracts with professional associations to handle the logistics, security, and such for their big conventions.

He told me he'd had an interesting conversation with a man from a local limousine service. The man said that New Orleans nearly ran of out limos for the convention. In fact, he was told, the NATPE convention—then probably hosting 10,000 attendees—always drew more limos than any other convention, even more than ones hosting attendees ten times as numerous. The limo demand for NATPE, he said, was so great that limo companies had to *import extra cars* from Baton Rouge and other nearby cities!

The message was clear. The demand for stretch limos is a reflection of stretch egos, and the television business topped all others in this category. More than the mere demand, he said that if an executive from XYZ network discovered that the limo of the person holding the same position at PQR network was larger than his/hers, that person would turn in the vehicle and demand one the same size or larger!

Think about it. People in Mainland America probably get to ride in a limo fewer than a handful of times in their lives, if they ever ride in one. Then, they see the Hollywood types demanding a limo at every major convention and insisting it be larger than their rival's. Hollywood excess doesn't sit well.

The Infamous Disney Memo

In 1991, when Michael Eisner was Chairman and Chief Executive Officer of The Walt Disney Company and Jeffrey Katzenberg was Chairman of Disney Studios, money flowed. Even though the Mouse House has a reputation for being one of the tightest in Hollywood, it still spills more money over lunch than most of the people between New York City and Los Angeles see in a lifetime.

In January of 1991, Katzenberg created "the memo," a 28-page analysis of the state of the motion picture industry. According to Larry Rohter of the *New York Times*, he railed against "runaway costs and mindless competition" and called on Disney and others to cut costs and end the lavish spending. He railed against financial excess.

The response was a case study in unintended consequences. Other studio heads ridiculed it. Eisner accused Katzenberg of stealing copy from a memo he had written while at Paramount. But some of the most violent reactions came from Disney employees who saw the missive as colossal hypocrisy by their leaders. They knew the kinds of salaries that Eisner and Katzenberg were pulling down. More than likely, there were a number of employees with Red State backgrounds and values about frugality and the responsible handling of money—or just a sense of fair play.

Some unknown person circulated a parody of the Katzenberg memo that had everybody but top Disney suits in stitches:

This country faces some of the worst economic and political conditions imaginable. Our streets are filled with the homeless, the uneducated; our troops face the constant threat of chemical weapons, Scud missiles, and repeated shell fire; and attendance at our parks is down, way down.

That's the bad news. Now, the good news. We intend to save money by paying our employees even less . . . . Our great and noble leader, Michael Eisner himself, took home a paltry $11 million in stock and salary this year, down from last year's haul of over $50 million. That's a 78 percent sacrifice!

All I'm asking is that each of you make the same sacrifice that Michael Eisner has made. By reducing employees' salaries by 78 percent, we will establish a platform to launch the next round of good times.[4]

Financial Obscenity

The memo's sarcasm was biting, and the point was clear. The excessive remuneration of Hollywood bosses gave them no moral foundation from which to preach frugality to the industry, and certainly not to their employees. Outside Movieland, the conservatives view such salaries of corporate leaders—in and out of Hollywood—as completely unthinkable and obscene.

The same goes for actors who get five to ten million dollars for eight weeks of work on a feature film or two million dollars an episode for a TV series. The same goes for athletes who get paid a million dollars a month for merely playing a game, and attorneys who get $350 an hour. The logic is, "Nobody's time and talent is worth that much," especially if the investment is not backed by something uniquely special in effort, skill, and education such as is needed to be a brain surgeon or rocket scientist. I use those two examples, because what happens in film and TV creation is commonly referred to in the industry as "not brain surgery" or "not rocket science." True, and rocket scientists and brain surgeons couldn't dream of raking in money like some in media's top echelons.

I had a conversation with a very successful TV producer who had four series on one of the big three networks at the same time. I asked him if his income was sufficient to compensate him for the overwhelming pressure and hassles that doing that many shows at once created. He didn't have a life. He said, with a big laugh, "I just get four obscene salaries instead of one!" I responded that my salary had never reached the level of "obscenity"—probably not even "mild indecency."

So it is with a couple hundred million more fiscally conservative Americans who steward every dollar to a make a financially secure life. They hold the money madness—dare I say greed—of Hollywood in contempt. I can't imagine how the truly poor view this excess.

Waste Not, Want Not

My parents were products of an Ohio farming community and the Great Depression. Both experiences left a deep imprint on their character . . . for good. They were particularly careful about avoiding waste. My mom often said, "A woman can throw out more in a teaspoon, than a man can bring in in a shovel." Thus, we saved and reused everything of value. Even a dab of leftovers got saved for later. They remembered childhood winters in depression years when they nearly starved.

While more recent generations do not see waste through those lenses, there is still a pretty strong ethic about frugality and being a "good steward" of money in Middle America. It explains, in large measure, the Sam Walton and Walmart success. That empire is built by millions of Red State people who will drive five miles to Walmart, and then use a 75¢ off coupon.

For many, this virtue is rooted in their faith, the Judeo-Christian teaching and tradition. In the Hebrew Scriptures, King Solomon's Book of Proverbs exhorts readers to "go to the ant" who lays up reserves for lean times (Proverbs 30:25). Jesus used a compelling parable about three men who were given custody of differing amounts of money. The one who did not steward wisely what he was given was condemned, and his money was taken and given to the man who had stewarded his money the best and gained the best return on his investment (Matthew 25:14-30).

Now, transition in your mind to the red carpet at the Academy Awards. As the lovelies are interviewed about their finery, they are often asked, "Who is your designer?" At this point, there is a kind of name-dropping gamesmanship among them. Out come the big names in world fashion. I've never heard a woman say, "I got it off the rack at Penneys." All well and good. But every woman in America knows that that name dropping is like the ring of a cash register—with numbers similar to the cost of their family sedan . . . or higher.

A friend told me of one of Hollywood's leading film directors who was on a shoot in Hawaii when a very severe storm threatened the islands. The production crew was advised to get to the mainland as soon as possible to avoid possible disaster. The director, even with an impending emergency, felt it beneath him to a fly on a commercial airline. He always flew in private jets. So the studio had to charter an available jumbo jet just for him and his entourage. Ka-ching. Ka-ching. Imagine the cost for a handful of people.

Here Comes the Bride . . . and Her Invoice

Then, these same Middle America women—for whom $175,000 would buy their family home—read the price tags on celebrity weddings in the tabloids.

There they learn . . .

- Donald Trump and Melanie Knauss spent $500,000 on wedding flowers.
- Brad Pitt and Jennifer Aniston spent $300,000 on lobster and champagne.
- Madonna and Guy Ritchie's wedding cost $1.5 million, as did Pierce Brosnan and Keely Shays Smith's.
- Victoria Adams' Vera Wang gown cost $100,000 for her marriage to David Beckham. (That's a pretty high price per wear!)
- Nicole Kidman and Keith Urban spent $80,000 on party favors—Tiffany clocks.[5]

I understand fully that "waste" is very relative. In a world where more than half of the people live on less than $300 a year, everyone reading this is "obscenely wealthy" and guilty of "waste." I am. But the lavish spending of the Hollywood set is far out of the realm of defensibility, at least to those in the middle—and poorer—levels of society.

Easy Come, Easy Go

I've been told first-person stories of the media mogul whose yacht cost him $15,000 every time he fueled its twin tanks. It had a pool and a helipad on it, too. No need to mention the purchase price of the 100' beauty, its full-time crew, its docking fees, etc.

Then, there are the villa-in-Rome and the chateau-in-France folks. For most Americans—who view themselves as blessed to have a 3-2 on a third acre and be within 10 years of mortgage payoff—this thinking is totally bizarre. Why would anyone want to own and maintain more than one home—even if money were no object?

I met a woman who was a domestic employee for a billionaire media mogul who had at least *five* homes in various parts of the world, one of which reportedly cost him $44 million. The multi-acre abode where she was employed saw the man and his family approximately six weeks a year.[6]

One of my first encounters with a studio executive in 1980, was with a production auditor at a major studio. He was squeaky clean in ethics and very professional in his job of tracking where the money went on the film productions of his studio. This is not an easy job on, say, a $100 million picture with thousands of contracts and individual costs.

He told me that a man showed up at the studio seeking to sell a computer software product that he envisioned would revolutionize the challenge of tracking movie production expenses. The man had taken software for huge construction projects like skyscrapers and adapted it to parallel track all the varied expenses of moviemaking.

The product, I was told, was a total nonstarter. Nobody in Hollywood wanted it. The auditor explained why. "No producer wants that kind of accountability on how he spends studio money. He couldn't put his mistress on the production payroll as a 'script assistant.'"

He told of a producer who had a brand new Mercedes damaged in a production crash scene, rather than using a less expensive car or a

Mercedes with a nice body, but totaled, from a scrap yard. In cahoots with the scrap dealer, the producer had the car sold for a few hundred dollars for scrap, then bought it back personally from the scrap yard owner with a nice commission for the dealer. Then, with the body work done on it, he had a $60,000 car for a fraction of the price.

Flower Flight

An executive at a legendary studio told me of a frustrating experience he had during his sixteen-year tenure at the company. In charge of contracts for movie productions, he had scheduled the studio jet six weeks in advance for use by a film star whose schedule needed it to meet production demands. The exec called a couple of days before the appointment to confirm the schedule and was told, "The jet is already booked."

My friend was stunned. "What do you mean, it's already booked? I made this reservation six weeks ago."

"Sorry, [the studio head] booked it." Of course, he took priority.

Checking into what had happened, the exec found out that the boss wasn't flying on the corporate jet. Neither was any other star or honcho of the studio. The chairman had the jet filled with flowers from a Beverly Hills florist to be flown round trip to England as a gift for his mistress.

I know these are extreme cases. They are. But cut the numbers in these stories in half. Reduce the parameters by 75 percent. They still will bring cries of "Foul!" from the masses of Americans who are "conservative," because they believe deeply in "conserving" money and everything of value.

Preoccupation with the Insignificant

In a world of excess—where a transatlantic flight filled with flowers for a mistress is no big deal—there is a strong tendency to focus more and more on things of less and less ultimate significance. This is true of entire societies of "haves" contrasted with societies of "have-nots." For instance, if your daily preoccupation is finding food for yourself or your family, difficulty with your cable TV provider really isn't on your radar.

On the converse, if you have all of your basic needs covered without question and have abundant resources to fulfill even most of your wants and luxuries, extremely insignificant things can become important to you in the most perverse kinds of ways.

A stunning example of this preoccupation with the insignificant is the special issue of *The Hollywood Reporter (THR)* I received recently. *The Hollywood Reporter*, along with *Variety*, is one of the two leading trade publications for insiders in the entertainment industry. This issue was the usual slick ten-by-thirteen-inch size and was the typical length, seventy pages. But, instead of containing the usual information about the goings on in the business of film, television, and new media, this issue was dedicated completely to watches! You read that right, an entire issue of beautiful graphics, gorgeous full page ads, and well-crafted copy about wristwatches.

One of the more compelling articles—hyped on the cover—was, "Hollywood Style: Who's Wearing What—Execs, an Agent, and a TV Chef Tell All about Their Timepieces." Then, there was the "Buyer's Guide 101: The Season's Top Ten Trends" and "Expert Tips for Your First High-End Purchase." There was the story of movie star Don Cheadle who "went from a kid's Timex to collecting top watchmaker Audemars Piguet." *THR* writers poured their research, talent, and wit into stories about watches to wear under water, the trend toward gray watch dials, Gatsby-style pieces ("all the rage again"), and how to start a collection of vintage watches. Photos of movie stars through the decades were selected to show their beautifully adorned wrists.[7]

Did I Miss Something Here?

Forgive my incredulity, but in this age of ten-dollar quartz watches which keep time within a few seconds a year, what gives the style of watch a person wears this kind of gravitas? And, I haven't talked about prices.

In a followup issue of *THR*, the mag hyped the "Supercharged Watch. Inspired by the iconic '70's Lamborghini Miura, MB&F's just-released HM5 features a louvered top to mimic the car's rear-and-side-facing display that's easy to read while driving. It's limited to only sixty-six pieces; $63,000."[8] Watches shown in the special issue included one worn by 007 Roger Moore in *Live and Let Die* which sold at $231,800 and Steve McQueen's Tag Heuer timepiece worn in the 1971 movie *Le Mans* which sold for $790,000. Seven hundred ninety thousand dollars for a wristwatch while millions on the planet are without food and shoes? A wristwatch is, after all, designed to provide easy access to what time it is. Millions in the Red States could think of better ways to spend or invest nearly eight hundred grand than by buying an instrument for portable time-telling. You think?

Substances—High Times in Hollywood

As I was writing this chapter, actor Charlie Sheen, star of *Two and a Half Men,* made the news through leaks from those who attended a 36-hour party he had. The reports were that the party was a day and a half orgy of sex and drugs featuring two porn stars and other female guests. At one point, it was reported, a man showed up at the door with an entire briefcase full of cocaine. I have no idea what a briefcase of cocaine costs, but it may be more than most people's annual salary. I don't know that any of the story is true, but I've met so many people in media whose lives or lives of family members have been destroyed by drug abuse that I am tempted to believe it. The cost of Charlie Sheen's cocaine was no problem for him. At the time, he was making about two million dollars *per episode* of his series. But, that's not the point. Drug use and abuse are two dynamics that seem to be socially acceptable in Hollywood.

Drug use is *not* socially acceptable in the Moral Center of America. Folks there don't "get" the lip service to anti-drug messages such as "Just Say 'No,'" but the more-or-less obvious acceptance of it in Hollywood. It should be noted that drug use seems to be much more common among the "creatives" than among the "suits." It makes sense that you can't run multibillion-dollar companies while high.

A cursory online search turned up lists of "100 Celebrities Arrested for Drug Possession," "Top 20 Drug-Induced Celebrity Deaths," and a list of approximately 170 "Famous Celebrities Who Have Been in Rehab." There is little overlap in the lists, and, remember, these lists include only those with enough name recognition to be dubbed "celebrities."[9] Ninety percent of the names on the lists were in entertainment with the rest in sports or other areas of public life. It could be assumed that for every name well-known enough to make the list there are ten or more entertainment professionals not recognizable enough to make the list. It is also safe to say that literally thousands in the relatively small media community are, or have been, involved in some form of drug and/or alcohol abuse.

From time to time, I see posted in business establishments notices like, "We test for drugs. If you use, don't apply." In three decades, I have never heard of any entertainment company deploying drug testing in employment. I'm sure some do, but I've not found any that put it "out front," if they do.

While far from an expert on drug use in Hollywood, *Performers* actress Megan Fox says Hollywood is awash in drugs. She admitted to *Maxim* magazine that she had experimented with a variety of drugs in the past, but not currently. "I know about five people who aren't on drugs today, and I'm one of them."[10]

"Where's the Stuff?"

In the eighties, I met the owner of a high-end recording studio right in the heart of Hollywood. He was a devout Christian, and his excellence had propelled his small studio into the top ranks of recording for some of America's leading rock and pop groups. But, he explained, "I don't know how much longer I can continue to see the success I've had for the last few years."

He had booked one of America's top bands, and when they arrived for the recording session, one of the band members asked, "Where's the stuff?"

My friend played dumb. "What do you mean?"

"C'mon, man, you know what I mean. Where's the stuff?"

"We don't provide that here."

Disgusted, the group never used the studio again. My friend explained that Hollywood recording studios were quietly expected to provide complimentary drugs to performers as part of the deal for recording studio contracts. Not willing to compromise his convictions or break the law, my friend watched his business wane and eventually go bankrupt.

Don't get me wrong. Every community and every industry has individuals who are drug and alcohol abusers. But imagine the crisis in America if the percentage of users, abusers, and those in rehab in politics, education, or in medicine were similar to the proportion in the entertainment industry. Scary thought.

Imagine, too, if the percentage of people in a single community the size of the entertainment industry (200,000?) took as casual an approach to drugs as Hollywood and engaged in the sort of "wink-wink" approach to its use and abuse common here. It would spell community disaster. No community in the Red States would tolerate such a thing. Their leaders would "just say no."

Conservative Morality vs. Hollywood Sex-cess

Contrary to popular perceptions from the moral left, moral conservatives are not enemies of sex. Even evangelical Christians include material on sexual fulfillment in their couples retreats, pre-marriage seminars, and biblical teaching. In fact, *the Song of Solomon,* a book in the Hebrew Scriptures/Old Testament, is very sensual literature glorifying the joys of sex in a committed love relationship.

The people in the Moral Middle States just hate the way current film, TV, and internet sites have demeaned what they consider a gift from God to enrich the personal, emotional, and even spiritual lives of those who exercise it in a covenant bond between a man and a woman. They are not against ice cream, either. They just know that excessive consumption of the stuff is destructive to one's well being—and lethal if you are diabetic. The way Hollywood people model and writers and producers portray sex is enraging to them, because they know the destruction that comes from it. Furthermore, their perspective is not just rooted in tradition or in archaic notions from religious strictures. It is a matter of their Judeo-Christian commands—a matter of their relationship with their God!

The joke going around Hollywood Is that Moses came down off Mount Sinai and reported to the Israelites, "Well, I have good news and bad news. The good news is that I negotiated God down from twenty commandments to ten. The bad news is that adultery is still on the list." Chuckle, chuckle.

Not so funny to conservative Jewish, Christian, and even Muslim adherents, because they recognize that God's commandments were not given to spoil our fun. They were given to enrich the lives of the obedient in ways unimaginable to the morally lawless. So, they go ballistic when they see the "marriage act," as it has traditionally been called in Catholic and Protestant communities, dragged into orgies of excess. As they watch Hollywood lead the way for the exercise of intimacy from one beloved spouse in a lifelong commitment to anybody who will crawl into bed ("hook up") with you, from a person of the opposite sex to any combination of same sex, bi-sex, underage sex, and even animal sex, they are outraged.

Their outrage is focused on these messages not only because they, as adults, just "don't buy them," they see what these messages are doing to the innocence and virtue of their kids. They don't want their kids' lives to end up the way the lives of celebrities and their multi-spouse, multi-sex, multi-lover "families" do.

Nothing Like a Pretty Face

When Charles Fleming penned *High Concept: Don Simpson and the Hollywood Culture of Excess*, he chronicled the excesses of the Hollywood lifestyle. Built around the rise and fall of film producer Don Simpson, there is a heartbreaking section on Don's attempts to keep his youthful looks and sex drive, both of which had been wasted by his life of dissipation more than by his age. He died at 53 of an overdose. Simpson once said, "The truth is, the more attractive you are, the easier life is. That's just the way it is."[11]

Fleming says of Simpson:

> Simpson gradually lost perspective on his physical appearance and continued experimenting with cosmetic surgery until he resembled an inflated ball of Naugahyde . . .. As the cosmetic procedures continued, Simpson at last began to resemble nothing so much as the chiseled, cartoon super heroes he'd obsessed over as a teenage comic book fanatic.[12]

And Simpson was a Hollywood *man!* A prominent West Los Angeles plastic surgeon says as many as one-third of his clients are now men. Simpson even had testosterone implants in his buttocks to increase his sex drive. When the procedure failed, the drug caused him to be aggressive to the point of violence.[13]

Testosterone was just one in a witches brew he had put into his body. The autopsy done after he died said the cause of death was "combined effects of multiple drug intake." His drug regimen was Toradol injections daily for pain, Librium to control mood swings, Ativan every six hours for agitation, Valium every six hours for anxiety, Depakote every six hours to counter "acute mania," Thorazine every four hours for anxiety, Cogentin for agitation, Vistaril and Lorazepam both every six hours for anxiety plus seventeen other drugs! Obviously, the consequences of Simpson's excesses could not be hidden by cosmetic procedures or by ingesting an entire pharmacy of drugs.[14]

It would be a waste of space to describe the near addiction of Hollywood *women* to cosmetic surgery with breast augmentation and face lifts leading the popular procedures. It's not uncommon to learn of plastic surgeons in Hollywood who have done tens of thousands of procedures each. Some of the sorriest sights in Filmland are women who will never see seventy again cut and pasted to look like twenty somethings and dressed like ladies of the evening. Even worse, a few are the victims of botched cosmetic surgeries, women whose faces and bodies vaguely resemble those in horror films.

Considering that breast augmentation costs from a low of $7,000 to $20,000 or more, this is another excess which people in Middle America consider outrageous and a testimony to unbridled insecurity and vanity, even if affordable.

Then, There's Paris

In *The Mirror Effect: How Celebrity Narcissism is Seducing America*, by Dr. Drew Pinsky and S. Mark Young,[15] the authors sound the alarm about the effect of Hollywood excess on the culture. Neither author comes at the subject from a moralistic or a religious perspective. Also, it would be hard to pin a "moral conservative" button on "Dr. Drew" in view of the sexually explicit nature of his TV shows like *Loveline* and *Celebrity Rehab with Dr. Drew*.

The concern of the two authors is the effect of narcissism-caused Hollywood excess on the American populace, especially teenagers. Drew and Young include a clinical definition of narcissism and describe its symptoms: mood disturbances, difficulty maintaining relationships, high likelihood of drug and alcohol abuse, an unhealthy drive to seek fame and fortune, a sense of entitlement, a need to exercise control over others, exhibitionism, exploitation, self-sufficiency to the point of collaborative inability, lack of empathy, and vanity.[16] Not a pretty package of attributes, but it does sound a bit like many of the celebrity class.

I was in line to enter the gate at the Paramount Studio lot once, and heard a woman in the line next to me screaming at the security guard, "Don't you know who I am?!? I'll have you fired!" Narcissism is marked by the "Don't-you-know-who-I-am?" syndrome. Judging from the age of the screaming woman, the security guard may have been way too young to know who she was, if she was ever really *somebody.*

Pinsky's book cites case studies of psychological narcissism and names names as examples. Paris Hilton plays a continuing role as a prime exhibit. Perhaps her own statement sums up her fit for the diagnosis: "There's nobody in the world like me. I think every decade has an iconic blonde—like Marilyn Monroe or Princess Diana—and right now, I'm that icon."[17]

I think the Real People in America see through that kind of talk and behavior from celebrities. However much they may find the peccadilloes of the famous fascinating, they know, down deep, most celebrities are sad souls. Pinsky confirms this. He says, " I can see the pain or illness that underlies their behavior, and it is heart-wrenching for me to watch what they are doing to themselves and how the public reacts . . .. Most of the people I see are very sick indeed."[18] Compounding the empathy they need, Pinsky says the *"fundamental source* [emphasis added] of pathological narcissism" is "childhood trauma."[19] There is a maxim that says, "Hurting people hurt people," and Hollywood celebrity biographies are replete with stories of tortured childhoods which explain much of their adult maladjustment. As a friend says, "Hollywood has taken the fun out of dysfunction."

Hef and the "Bunny Hutch"

Let me wrap up this chapter on excess with a few observations about "Hef." Born Hugh Marston Hefner in 1926, "Hef" is known globally for his lifestyle and his soft porn empire known as Playboy. He is lesser known for his hard-core pornography businesses like Spice Digital Networks, Club Jenna, and adult.com.[20] Much of Hefner's success has been achieved by exploiting the sexual fantasies of men around the world and, simultaneously, exploiting women—despite what he says. His airbrushed nudes, rotating harem of personal sex partners, Playboy Mansion orgies, and his championing of the "Playboy Philosophy" have given him global recognition. The Playboy bunny is probably a recognizable brand second only to Coca Cola around the world.

But, is Hef admired and viewed as iconic on Main Street? If so, the residents on Main haven't gotten beneath the airbrushing. Do an internet search of the dark secrets of the Playboy mansion, former Playmates' stories, and Hef's own private reputation for paid abortions, regular multi-partner orgies at the mansion, and the like. If you do this, the glossy cover of his life disappears like a rain-soaked edition of his magazine.

I've only met Hefner once, but a friend who interviewed him in depth for a TV series found him a sad and sorry person searching for love and—despite multitudes of lovers—not finding it. It's too late now for the octogenarian to take this approach to life, but I wouldn't trade my half-century-plus love relationship with the wife of my youth and the blessings of a right-living, intact family for Hef's successes and excesses. Knowing the dark side of his life, the majority of the Flyovers wouldn't trade either.

Those in the heartland can see where Hollywood excesses end up. They create an even wider chasm between entertainment's gods of Mammon and Glitz and the True and Living God who is largely revered by the people who live between JFK and LAX.

CHAPTER TEN

"YOU MAKE NO SENSE!"

The Conflict over Rationality

Slicing and Dicing with Words

Winston Churchill and Lady Nancy Astor were political and personal rivals in England. In 1919, Lady Astor was the first woman to sit as a Member of Parliament (MP) in the British House of Commons, and Churchill was not at all happy that a woman had invaded the Parliament "men's club." Churchill is reported to have told Lady Astor that having a woman in Parliament was like having a woman intrude on him in the bathroom. Lady Astor replied, "You're not handsome enough to have such fears."

In one of the more famous interchanges between the two, Lady Nancy Astor said, "Winston, if you were my husband, I'd poison your tea." Churchill retorted, "Nancy, if I were your husband, I'd drink it."[1]

A similar exchange among MPs occurred between Lord Beaconsfield (Benjamin Disraeli) and William Gladstone. The two were exceptional politicians, but they absolutely loathed each other. On one occasion, Disraeli said, "The difference between a misfortune and a calamity is this: If Gladstone fell into the Thames, it would be a misfortune. But if someone dragged him out again, that would be a calamity."[2]

It was clear that Churchill and Astor and Disraeli and Gladstone could not come to the other's point of view. So, they engaged in running battles of words with witty, but mean-spirited, exchanges. When they didn't have evidence or logic or cogent arguments on their side, they attacked each other's *persons*.

This is typical dialogue when people are behaving badly. I reference it here because this kind of "word war" has marked the intercourse between Media World and American people of faith for much of the past 100 years of the entertainment business. The only difference between the war of words in British Parliament and in the Hollywood culture wars is that the Tinseltown/Faith-Community version isn't nearly so witty. Furthermore, it seems to have become more vitriolic in the last fifteen years.

"He Called Me a 'Monster'!"

I sat in the office of the head of a major cable network years ago, a man who is still a trusted Jewish friend. We had not been together for a while, and after getting reacquainted, he said, "I was clicking through the channels the other day, and came upon a show with Pat Robertson. You know what he did? He called me a 'monster'!" My friend was enraged. "How dare he call me that. He's never met me. If he has an issue with me, why doesn't he come in here like you do and sit down, so we can talk. But for him to go on his show and call me a monster . . . ." The exec is a very principled, God-fearing man, and the insult obviously cut deep.

"Would you really sit down with him? I think I might be able to arrange it."

"Absolutely. But, for him to call me a 'monster' . . . "

The offense was justified. The back story is that my friend's network was part of a huge conglomerate of media companies. One of the other companies under the corporate umbrella had released some product that Robertson found offensive . . . with good reason. But Pat had generalized his attack to the executives of the entire conglomerate and leveled this vicious assault on them all on his TV show.

"They Called Us 'Fascists'!"

Joe Scarborough of MSNBC had a feature on his show asking the question, "Why is it okay to attack God and Christians?" In his show commentary, Scarborough noted that it seems that a cottage industry has developed which puts out books, film documentaries, and blogs that demean Jesus Christ, attack those who believe in Him, and slander Christian believers.

On his list of offenses, he noted that *Titanic* director James Cameron filmed a special seeking to prove that Jesus was a fraud and Christianity a hoax. *The Da Vinci Code* movie and book told a fictional story—with the impression that it was fact—that undermined most of the basic tenets of the Christian faith. Then, too, a number of hot-selling books attack Christians or their beliefs: *The God Delusion, Kingdom Coming: The Rise of Christian Nationalism,* and *American Fascists: The Christian Right and the War on America.* Did you get that? Fascists. *Losing Moses on the Freeway: The Ten Commandments in America* and *Letter to a Christian Nation* describe Christians as "murderously intolerant," "yearning for apocalyptic violence," and "fevered by religious radicalism."[3] Most ministers would break out in hives with excitement if their parishioners were even ten percent as motivated for *anything* as the above characterizations suggest. Getting the spiritual slugs and "frozen chosen" out of the pews is a much greater challenge than reigning in their "murderous yearnings" or "fevered radicalism"!

If it seems over the top to you to have responsible media executives called "monsters" and the Christian devout dubbed "fascists" and "murderously intolerant," you can get a sense of the irrationality of the dialogue between those screaming their own form of obscenities at each other across the cultural divide.

Point Weak. Shout Louder.

When I was in seminary, a professor told of a minister whose sermon notes contained the marginal note, "Point weak. Shout louder." It has occurred to me that this principle has become almost typical of the intercourse between the point people in media and the firebrands of the Faith Community. Leaders on both sides have sought to bolster their lack of facts and hard evidence with nuclear rhetoric. Actually, maybe that statement is incorrect. In the feelings culture—part of contemporary postmodernism—maybe facts and hard evidence mean nothing anyway.

Exhausted at a trade convention from pounding the concrete of Las Vegas streets, hotels, and exhibit halls for three days, I collapsed into an overstuffed chair in a lounge area. There was a well-scrubbed gentleman in the chair next to me, so we got acquainted. We had a lot in common—similar age, Ph.D.s from major universities, etc. He headed a media company with a unique niche in the marketplace and described it for me. When he heard that I headed an organization that consults with media execs on the Christian community, he was fascinated.

It soon became appropriate, I thought, to ask him if the good doctor had any personal faith. There was a prompt "no." I asked if he had any belief in God and got the same "no." When I asked why this was the case, he gave an answer that surprised me in its candor, "God doesn't make any sense to me."

This was clearly not a time or setting in which I was motivated to "shout louder." Besides, I don't have one scintilla of question that my worldview "makes sense." But I walked away from that interchange with the awareness that the great chasm between Hollywood and prime-value Americans is as enormous as it is because each believes the other's viewpoints "make no sense."

Origins, for Starters

Over lunch in a nice Manhattan restaurant, I met with a friend of about eight years. We originally met on a company cold call when he was a top exec at one of the big three TV networks. He is, at best, an agnostic and has been intrigued by, but not convinced of, my God-centered worldview. He has real doubts about the existence of any kind of higher power.

Early in the conversation, he began raving about an I-Max film he'd seen of the universe, *Hubble 3-D*. He was rhapsodizing about the spectacular scenes of the glories of the universe from black holes to galaxies, from quasars to the Milky Way. I listened attentively until he wound down and then hit him with what I thought was an appropriate question.

"So, how do you think all these marvels of the universe happened?"

He had a momentary sick look on his face as if the Christian had just launched a "gotcha," and then admitted that he didn't know, but it probably just happened.

"So," I said, "let me see if I can capture your view of the universe accurately. First, there was nothing. Then, the nothing exploded. When it exploded, it resulted in all of these incredible things you are describing with only chance factors involved—no intelligence or design."

The dialogue after that was animated, and I left my friend thinking of his cosmology, "It makes no sense at all. This view is totally irrational."

Obviously, he thinks that believing in some supreme being big enough and powerful enough to have created the universe is sheer idiocy. Trust me, more people in America's heartland believe this idiocy than those in the urban fringes of our nation, LA and NYC. In the research my organization sponsored by America's Research Group (ARG), 96.2 percent of Christians surveyed believed in a creator, not evolution![4]

To the non-media masses, it takes more faith to believe in the wonders of the cosmos happening by chance than by an Omnipotent Designer. We are galaxies apart . . . pun intended.

But Hollywood producers keep putting out product that assumes a non-divine origin to all that exists. In so doing, they alienate the masses of the faith-full for whom this notion is secular foolhardiness.

The chasm deepens.

Darwinism Has Evolved

Then, there is the primate-to-man hypothesis and Darwin's evolutionary tree. Have we not all seen the chart showing creatures linked from a single cell in some primordial ooze into finned, then footed, then winged, and then upright walking creatures?

Those creationists who are viewed as imbeciles by the scientific world aren't so sure about Darwinism. Never mind there is no procreation between species, not even among creatures so similar as cats and dogs. Never mind that DNA is showing no link between major species on the Evolutionary Tree. Never mind that mutation—the major mechanism for significant evolutionary change in Darwinism—has never been shown to be constructive, because mutant forms are typically impaired. Never mind that even mechanisms within a single cell are so complex as to defy the notion of "design" by *chance*. Never mind that DNA itself is more complicated than man's most intricate computer software programming. Never mind that the Cambrian era of the earth's fossil record holds a virtual explosion of complicated life forms with no evidence of simple-to-complex forms in older strata as Darwinism would require.

But clearly, the world of media buys Darwinism without question as a matter of nearly blind faith. It is an assumed explanation in documentaries and story lines throughout the film and TV world. Doubting Darwin in Hollywood and New York circles is flat-earth thinking.

Interestingly, according to *Time* magazine, 60 percent of American's high school biology teachers don't believe Charlie D's hypotheses, despite being educated in major universities where it was unanimously taught as gospel truth. They teach them "only as they pertain to molecular biology, as one alternative among a variety of theories . . . or as necessary to pass national tests."[5]

To people in the Red States, Darwinism makes no sense. One more escarpment separating the two sides.

Pro-Choice? Of course.

Is there any reason to elucidate the charges of irrationality being lobbed across the vast divide on the issue of abortion?

We've heard Hollywood's message in word and on celluloid: "Those pro-life zealots who bomb abortion clinics and murder pro-choice doctors—described as if this is standard operating practice—have the audacity to interpose the government, or worse, their religious beliefs between a woman and her 'POC,' product of conception. What unmitigated gall! How could one get more irrational in one's thinking?" And, then, to postulate that a woman considering abortion should be required to learn more about the process and the result—viewing a sonogram of the fetus, seeing a film of a real abortion, or hearing from women who have experienced the procedure—is considered an outrage. The proportion of Hollywood illuminati showing up in pro-choice parades and marches and making pro-choice statements and commercials I would guess to be 100 to 3 to those who are pro-life.

From the other side, the above learning experiences would seemingly assist in making a more informed "choice," one with full awareness of the seriousness of the decision to the mother, her fetus, and her family. The Middle America folks think there are other facts which seem irrefutable: The POC is going to become a human being, even before it is "viable." It has a beating heart and the ability to feel pain in the womb at an early stage. It is, by every known definition, "a living organism," even a *human* organism.

Furthermore, the "choice" concept is seldom backed up to the procreative act. How about "choosing" not to have sex if a child is not wanted? What would be wrong with "choosing" to bring an unwanted young life into the world and providing it to a childless couple in a long line of would-be adoptive parents? These suggestions are viewed as assaults on the "reproductive rights" of a woman by what pro-lifers call the "pro-aborts." But, this thinking makes complete sense to what is now statistically the majority of Americans with only 42 percent now considering themselves pro-choice, according to Gallup.[6] These more conservative Americans are the same people who don't understand why federal law should provide up to $5,000 in fines and a year in prison for destroying a bald eagle.[7] Yet, there is no fine nor imprisonment for crushing babies' skulls and dismembering their bodies *in utero* to accommodate "choice."

What a black-hole-sized void between the two sides!

And God Created Adam and Steve

One example of the rhetoric in the fight between entertainment industry spokespersons and the Judeo-Christian majority is the above title line pulled from the placard of a "pro-family" street protester against gay marriage, "God didn't create Adam and Steve."

But, President George W. Bush's 29-year-old daughter, Barbara, expressed the opposing viewpoint well when she did a commercial for a New York pro-gay-marriage group, New Yorkers for Marriage Equality. "Everyone should have the right to marry the person that they love. Join us."[8] To the vast majority of those in film, television, and the media, gay rights and gay marriage are not complicated issues. The matter is as simple as Barbara's statement. It's about equality, equal rights. It's about justice. It's about nondiscrimination. It's about the American ethos of freedom and fair play. It's even about love. It's not complicated.

To the vast body of Americans who oppose the institutionalization of gay "rights" and gay marriage, both campaigns are completely irrational. The gay thing (1) isn't at all "gay," and (2) makes as little connective sense as two electrical plugs with no outlet . . . or vice versa. It's an assault on reason, Natural Law, and three thousand five hundred years of Judeo-Christian virtue. It's an attack on the nuclear family of one male, one female, and the offspring of their union. To assault the traditional family, to these folks, is to assault the single most significant component of society, the societal "glue," the institution which holds every society together. To institutionalize homosexual practice and union into law is to fly in the face of cultural mores which have been dominant not only in the western world, but in *all the world* in *all* of recorded history. It's even an assault on the faith of the world's three major religions. To believe otherwise is viewed as intentional denial possible only through the suspension of fact and reason.

In an industry in which the gays and lesbians are the single most powerful special interest group, and in which Broadway, dance, choreography, makeup, and a number of other industry segments are dominated by gays and lesbians, the support for the gay agenda is completely understandable. At the same time, most Americans view gay and lesbian behaviors as permissible under law in light of the nation's freedoms, but inherently repulsive and "immoral" personally. Missing this point, Hollywood pushes the gay agenda in person and in product and, thus, drives an even deeper wedge into the crevasse that separates the industry from the mainland masses—all this for a constituency of about four percent of the populus.[9]

And All the Rest . . .

The list could go on. We could examine the gulf between the two warring sides on traditional vs. cultic religious thinking, between anti-big-corporation vs. small-government-entrepreneur-friendly thinking, and between protection of the environment vs. economic development.

We could evaluate the definition of legitimate art and creativity which includes public sex-act "performance art," child pornography, and portrayals of Jesus Christ in urine. We could examine the legitimacy of music which uses the N-word and F-word, recommends the killing of cops, or advocates sexual abuse of women and girls.

No need. The point is made. On nearly every matter of public interest and personal preference there is a mountainous divide.

But what about the flag, motherhood, and apple pie? On the Hollywood side, the flag can legitimately be burned in public, motherhood is a slap at gay men who raise children in a legal union, and apple pie should most likely be outlawed in school lunches as contributing to obesity.

Someone has said, "People's opinions are like their watches. Each is different, yet each is sure his is correct." Nowhere is this more true than in the Hollywood/Flyover conflict. But in this mega-debate, not only are the other guy's viewpoints wrong, they are *insane* and *dangerous!*

CHAPTER ELEVEN

"SHOCK AND AWE"

The Emissaries of Peace Take up Arms

Tale of the Urundus

It was a horrifying discovery there in the steamy jungles of Gabunda Urundi. Never before reached by those from the outside world, the native tribe was discovered to be engaging in the most barbaric practices ever discovered in the history of anthropology and the search for ancient cultures.

The Urundu tribe was eating human flesh as more-or-less standard practice. When victims of the murderous warriors were mortally slain, their bodies were put on spits and roasted on an open fire for a great tribal victory feast. Sometimes, those deemed by the tribal council to be less war-worthy than others were given the dreaded mark of the cobra on the forehead and destined to die as food for the rest of the tribe at a later time. Even children were sacrificed for pagan feasts on every Blue Moon.

Christian missionaries from the U.S. and Europe living across the border from Gabunda Urundi learned of the awful practices of these demonic savages and decided they must do something. After a week of prayer and planning, they decided on a strategy. They would drop small, solar-powered audio devices carrying strongly-worded messages in the native tongue demanding that the barbaric practices of the tribe stop immediately . . . or else!

Dropped from small airplanes owned by the missionaries, the devices were picked up by the tribespeople, and the message came through loud and clear. The Urundus were being ordered to cease and desist from all their barbaric tribal practices and immediately surrender to forces which were waiting outside the parameters of the village to enter and take control. Urundu scouts had detected the presence of the outsiders before the rain of electronic messengers descended on the village.

As the devices were falling through the clouds, the missionaries marched a safe distance around the village with pictograph signs and loud shouts of "Gabba Nie Populi," which being translated from Urundese, declared, "Stop eating people!"

The hastily called tribal council meeting in the village was a testimony to the principle of unintended consequences. Not only did the native people not end their cannibalism nor surrender to the Anglo-European forces outside their region, they held a great war rally. They sharpened their spears and other weapons, donned their war paint, and appealed to their gods for victory over the arrogant enemies who presumed to tell them how to run their lives.

Wild War II

As the beat of village war drums and the familiar sounds of preparations for a slaughter of—and feasting on—their enemies grew louder, the missionary countenances reflected an eloquent "Oops!" message. The angst was greater when poison arrows began flying by the thousands over the tall forests in the direction of the moralistic protesters.

A second meeting of the Missionary Coalition met to reframe strategy. Obviously, this first one had failed. Arguments over the next strategy were intense. Then, one leader came up with strategy two: boycotts.

Very artistic handmade Urundu products had been coming out of the jungles through neighboring tribesmen who served as "wholesale distributors" for the Urundus. Beautiful beadwork, hand-carved totems, and the hides of rare animals were especially desirable at the trading posts far away. Income from these objects had become a major source of revenue for the Urundu people.

After some back-and-forth among the Christians, one missionary spoke. "I know, we'll boycott! The tribe can't survive without the revenue from their native crafts. Aha!"

The strategy was adopted by Coalition members over the objections of some who thought a less warlike approach might be in order—especially since the first confrontational strategy had been such a colossal failure. The minority was shouted down by a voice vote, and the boycott was mobilized.

Economic Sanctions

The middle men from the neighboring tribes were told that no purchases would be forthcoming of any Urundu craft objects. They were also informed that all trading post owners who handled Urundu items would be boycotted by all expatriates in the nation. This would be an economic disaster for the post owner/managers and the middle men.

The Urundu economy was unfazed. Urundus had been living off the land for millennia and didn't need the supplemental trinket income to survive. But the Urundu chief was apoplectic with rage at the continuing insults from the outsiders. Ordering his warriors to gather for a great victory rally, he had them take those solar audio devices and record a new message on each. When done, the devices were tied to warrior arrows and sent flying out of the village to the vicinity of the missionaries. Then, the warriors marched out to slaughter their foes.

As the war chants of the Urundus grew closer, and the sky drew darker with flying arrows, the righteous knew they had created Oops Number 2. When the missionaries listened to the message on each arrow, it announced, "Geheba nor fierobi" which, when translated, bore the message, "Go to hell!"

An Uncomfortable Application of the Parable

Obviously, the preceding story is fiction. But it isn't. The strategies deployed by the Christians in the parable are precisely the strategies that have been deployed against the media "Urundus" for a century—with very similar results.

In the meantime, some in the Christian camp have asked, "Is this really the way we should be approaching the Hollywood problem?" "What about our message of love and forgiveness?" "What about seeking to build some bridges to the leaders of media rather than driving them to erect higher walls?"

When delegates to the 11,000 member Southern Baptist Convention moved to establish a boycott of the Walt Disney Company in summer of 1996, the sentiment in favor of it at the convention was by no means unanimous. Pastors of some of the Convention's largest churches expressed their concerns that the approach was not in keeping with the Spirit of Christ, was going to be predictably ineffective, and even ". . . makes us look foolish."[1] On the floor of the convention before the vote, Rev. Rick Markham said, "In typical Baptist fashion, I am afraid, we have reacted to an extreme by positioning ourselves at another extreme."[2]

The Southern Baptists joined with Rev. Donald Wildmon's American Family Association and Dr. James Dobson's Focus on the Family organizations in the boycott which they called off after eight years in 2005. To their credit, these huge evangelical entities have deep convictions and were seeking a way to get a hearing and a response from what many in the Red States experience as an industry whose leaders are often totally deaf to concerns of conservatives. While I don't support the boycott strategy, I understand the frustration and feeling that "there was no other option left." Requests to sit down with leaders of Disney prior to the boycott apparently had been ignored. This is not an uncommon response for leaders in media who typically do not take seriously the concerns of the Flyovers. Michael Eisner's response in an interview on *60 Minutes* was classic. He said of the sponsors of the boycott, "They're nuts. They really are."[3]

There's My Foot [Bang!]

I learned of a classic case of deploying a counterproductive strategy. Years ago, NBC had a performer on *Saturday Night Live* who used the "F" word on the show. An NBC exec told me that—unbeknownst to the conservative attack dogs from the Christian community—the producers of the show had pretty much "had it up to here" with the offending actor. He had caused problems before, the network execs were tired of his shenanigans, and the decision was made by the NBC suits to fire him off the show.

At the same time, the conservatives who were enraged by the F-bomb mounted an assault on NBC demanding that the actor be fired. This changed the dynamics of NBC's decision drastically. If the execs followed through with the termination, they would appear to the public to be caving to the pressure of the Christian antagonists. Not willing to do that, and in so doing give credibility to the demands, NBC execs decided to give the actor one more chance. He stayed on the show.

Had the concerned Christians quietly and respectfully approached NBC with their concerns, their goal probably would have been achieved and the actor fired. As it turned out, it was their *method* which created the opposite result.

There is an expression that "If all you have is a hammer, everything looks like a nail." The anger strategies of moral conservatives have often worked against them in their dealings with media power brokers. Everything has looked to the hammer-wielders of the Faith Community as long slender spikes with broad flat heads just waiting to be banged. Wrong.

A Dirty Little Secret about Anger

Dr. Gene Scott, a Christian minister operating originally out of a small church and studio in Glendale, California, was unique, to say the least. If you ever saw Dr. Scott on TV, you never forgot him. You would remember one or more of the following images of the man:

- Scribbling his theological notions and outlines on blackboards jammed with scrawl which included Greek and Hebrew words from the Bible

- Bearded, sitting with his sunglasses on, smoking a cigar, wearing two or three hats at the same time, peering over his Bible, and demanding money with cessation of teaching until his call handlers indicated that enough money had come
- Seemingly out-of-place video footage of his stable of beautiful trained horses going through their paces as Scott waited for the audience to respond to his demand for contributions
- Exhortations lightly sprinkled with "hells" and "damns" to emphasize his points, a seeming contradiction for a "minister of the gospel"
- His consistent anger

Scott, now deceased, told a mutual friend that in the beginning, his little TV program was struggling along week after week with low viewership and miniscule donor response until, on one show, he got angry. He chewed out the viewers, raged against their noninvolvement, demanded that they support his ministry financially, and berated them for their lack of commitment.

He told my friend, "I was stunned. Money poured in. I knew, then, that if I was going to see results, I was going to have to be angry." Angry he was. A small army of loyal viewers/donors kept his program expanding and even enriched the man personally. His thoroughbreds and his Rolls Royce gave testimony to that.

Scott had discovered the dirty little secret of charitable fund raising: you have to get the donors' juices flowing. This is not unique to Christian fund raising. It is axiomatic to all fund raising. I've read Abe Foxman's fund letters for the Anti-Defamation League and those by the head of the NRA.

Politicians have to get you so angry at the awful things the opponent is doing that you dig deep to support their campaigns. Orphan-support charities have to get you deeply moved by the awful abuse, exploitation, and conditions of the poor orphans, or you won't sacrifice to build their new orphanage. Unions have to get you so ticked off at the antics of the greedy capitalists who run the company that you'll both pay the exorbitant dues and get out and march in the job actions. Charities that support abused women or children have to move you with stories of horrific abuse to get you to fund their annual campaigns.

A leading Christian fund raiser told me one time, "If you want donors to bleed, you have to hemorrhage."

Why Hollywood Hates Conservative Christians, Part I

When American Family Association founder and former head Donald Wildmon wrote his personal story, he titled the book *Don Wildmon: The Man the Networks Love to Hate*.[4] I guess that having drawn contempt from TV executives was, for Don, a badge of honor. I've never understood that thinking coming from a Christian. I've never felt more righteous when I've been hated. I've understood contempt for my beliefs and vocal denunciation of same, but I've always endeavored to be personally warm, gracious, and reasonable, even if my views drew violent and hateful responses.

Jesus' best friend, His follower John, described Jesus' communication style as follows: "The law was given through Moses; grace and truth came by Jesus Christ" (John 1:17). That rare mix of unvarnished truthfulness and, yet, personal graciousness has been a commonly missing element in the dialogue between Filmland and the Moral Middle. This lack of common courtesy, respect, and, yes, *grace* is, I believe, partly responsible for the chasm between the two worlds. When the verbiage generates more heat than light, there is more conflagration than illumination.

Barbaric communication is not limited to the discourse with Tinseltown leaders. It has become epidemic in many areas of public life. What, in politics, used to be "my worthy opponent" has become "my contemptible enemy." When public protesters carry placards for their cause, it is scary to note the number of references to Adolf Hitler when characterizing the figure heads on the other side of the issue. Sheer barbarism.

My grandma used to say, "You catch more flies with honey than you do with vinegar." Even with her fifth-grade education, she knew something that urbane, well-educated, professional people have forgotten. Certainly, there has been lack of grace in the speech of those on both sides of the media/mainland divide.

The "Goliath Factor"

If the importance of anger is powerful in mobilizing people and raising funds for a cause, there is a second dynamic that is equally powerful. It is having an identifiable giant to slay.

The leader of a Christian organization known for its stridency and its mobilizing of millions to condemn Hollywood's sins told a friend of mine, "Every David has to have a Goliath to slay." The man's actions over the years have become proof that he yearns for the appearance on the public scene of some blasphemous giant who can become a target for his five small stones. Being able to demonize some media leader or network or studio or mega-corporation is key to mobilizing the masses to act and to contribute.

I got a call one day from a friend in the executive ranks of a major television network. She was nearly beside herself. Her company was getting a thousand angry calls and emails *a day* from livid Christians! Knowing that our organization consults on the Christian community, she was calling for counsel.

The back story is that one of the network's on-air personalities had uttered a vile attack on Jesus while looped on vodka at a company party. Even though the incident was not aired and was never to be aired, reports of the incident hit the internet, and the fiery arrows came flying into the network headquarters. I agreed that our organization would help the network resolve the matter, and got information from her and her associates about the source of the irate responses.

I personally knew two of the three leaders who were fomenting the crisis for the network, and started making calls to them. In anticipation of the calls, I did my homework and discovered the following:

- The network had already issued a public apology.
- The network had the offending employee issue a public apology.
- One of the Christian organization's websites was falsely claiming that the network "had refused to take action" to the offense.

- The lead protest organization was demanding that the network immediately fire the offending employee.

To two of the network execs, I predicted that we would be successful in getting the email blitz under control. That happened. In one week, the email count dropped from 1000 to 5 a day. But I also predicted a "second wave," because I was sure the organization would rush into production a massive fund raising letter demonizing the network. I knew they would not miss the opportunity to muster the masses to help them fight this Goliath. Organizational funding was involved. The letter materialized as predicted. The second wave of emails didn't.

The Greater Offense?

Here is the crux of this conflict from an ethical perspective. In my animated phone conversation with the head of the lead protest organization, I confronted him on what I felt was a greater offense. The network was being pilloried for what one employee with too much bubbly said at a private dinner—an offense for which both the network and the employee issued a public apology. Was it right to hammer them?

The Christian organization had created a costly public relations nightmare for two very devout Christian executives and the heads of their very responsible TV network—one with a squeaky clean reputation for responsible programming. That same Christian organization had used a falsehood on its website to fuel the anger of its constituents. In demanding the termination of the apologetic employee, it showed no grace, understanding, or forgiveness for the individual involved. Was this in keeping with the Christian faith?

The defense I got from the head of the organization was, "Well, you know that if the offense had been against Jews or Muslims or blacks, she would have been fired." I countered that if our responses as followers of Jesus Christ were not driven by a higher standard than others, we had already lost a much greater area of moral high ground.

In the warfare between entertainment industry leaders and the morally sensitive people of faith in America, the conservative Christian community has often been willing to sacrifice reason, courtesy, respect, and grace to WIN THE BATTLE! I am convinced that WINNING THE BATTLE in the short term is often LOSING THE WAR, a long-term loss. Might there not be a time when it is better to be loving than to be so all-fired right? Might there not be a place for strategies motivated by reason and respect rather than by power plays and anger?

As one media exec told me, "For us 'angry Christian' is a redundancy. That's the only kind we know." What a shame.

Why Hollywood Hates Conservative Christians, Part II

So, leaders in media hate the moral conservatives because they don't show them respect and have majored in power-based "anger strategies" for decades. There are other reasons as well.

When you live inside a cultural cocoon—as many in religious Middle America do—you aren't able to see your own zits. Trust me, they have 'em. When our organization puts on its Corporate Seminar for execs in major media companies, the room gets really quiet when I outline the "weaknesses" of the devout. There is mild disbelief that (1) I can see them and (2) that I am willing to admit them. They are accustomed to neither from most of their religious critics.

Following are a few weaknesses that make what Hollywood derisively calls the "religious right" so contemptible.

- **Their separation from the culture for reasons of faith keeps them from communicating effectively with it or relating well to it.**

Conservative Christians joke among themselves that they have their own language: Christianese. They can give you an entire paragraph with in-house theological and cultural lingo that would be about as understandable to outsiders as Swahili. Outsiders find this weird. The response is, "They don't talk our language. How do they expect me to understand them?"

- **They can assume a "siege mentality" which makes them defensive, reactive, and even a bit paranoid.**

When those in Hollywood hear messages like "Take Back America" or those that label all non-evangelicals as "godless," they shudder. When they see mobilization of Christians to gain political power, they feel they have to mobilize. Remember, producer Norman Lear founded People for the American Way in large measure to counter the increasing power of the Moral Majority.

- **Those with the "Christian religion without the relationship" can be so doctrinaire as to be closed-minded and unthinking.**

A bumper sticker not uncommon in conservative Christian communities says, "God said it. I believe it. That settles it." When you think about it, the door to dialogue, reasonable inquiry, and open and honest interchange just got slammed in the face of all who don't agree with that message. While it may be true that "Some minds are so open, they need to be closed for repairs," it is also true that "Some minds are so closed that they need to be opened for fresh air." Believers who are secure in their faith and relying on a personal relationship with God rather than the strictures of the Christian "religion," can engage in nonconfrontational dialogue . . . and do so comfortably.

- **Their belief that they possess absolute Truth can cause them to be arrogant and condescending.**

Especially for those who believe that there are no absolutes and that morality is relative, the "I have ultimate Truth" statements or attitudes are a real turnoff—almost "fightin' words." If outsiders even detected a hint of "I could be wrong . . .," it would help them relate.

- **Their enthusiasm for the radical transformation of life they attribute to their faith can make them insensitive zealots in promoting their beliefs.**

It's wearisome to be in relationships with people who are "Johnny One-note." They only can talk about one subject. It's also a friendship killer to have someone incessantly talk about his faith or try to recruit you for his cause. It's like having a brother-in-law in a multilevel marketing business. You are never quite sure whether he is interested in you because you are family or because he wants to get you in his down line.

- **Their belief that their values are rooted in the Law of God can lead them to use their power to attempt to reform those who do not share their faith or values.**

To outsiders, this is really scary. Christians mobilizing political power so they can enforce their version of Sharia Law on the entire populace is Talibanic thinking. This is not the outsiders' vision of "religious freedom."

- **Their offense at violations of their ("God's") moral standards can cause them to attack the violating person rather than just condemn the behavior.**

This is a common dynamic on both sides—the inability to separate issues from persons. If there is a boycott of Disney, the chairman or CEO becomes the "enemy" or, at least, the fall guy. I once took the opportunity to apologize to Michael Eisner for the unkindness and lack of respect shown to him during the boycott of Disney/ABC by those calling themselves Christians. He seemed unsure how to handle the apology, but thanked me.

If media moguls have a bone to pick with the "religious right," then Jim and Tammy Baker, Jimmy Swaggert, and Ted Haggart are dragged to the stake to be burned as representative of the entire Faith Community.

Personalizing differences and demonizing the persons on the other side of the great divide lose more traction in the conflict than is gained, a lot more. Furthermore, it is wrong.

Boycotts, hate mail, protests, and anger strategies . . . the "shock and awe" approach didn't secure a victory in Iraq, and it most assuredly won't secure one for moral conservatives in the war with Hollywood.

Poet Robert Burns said in his Scottish dialect, "Oh wad some power the giftie gie us to see oursel's as others see us!" If moral conservatives want to know some of the reasons why Hollywood hates them, they might start by looking in the mirror. They can be really quite ugly.

CHAPTER TWELVE

"DON'T YOU KNOW WHO I AM?"

The Conflict over Entitlement

Poor Baby!

The setting was a Beverly Hills beauty salon. It was an ugly scene. A well-scrubbed woman adorned with typical symbols of wealth was throwing a hissy fit in front of her hairdresser. Loud enough for all in the salon to hear, the angry woman was railing against the domestic help who served her at her nearby mansion.

It appears that one of the servants was supposed to have washed the Rolls Royce prior to the lady's morning outing. When she went to the garage to leave on her errands, she discovered—lo, and behold—the Rolls was not washed and ready for her departure.

Furious, she explained that she had no other alternative but to drive the family Jaguar to her beauty shop appointment.

I am sure that you and I could think of worse catastrophes than this, but this one was big enough to spoil the self-obsessed matron's whole day. The issue was clear. She was *entitled* to have whatever car she wanted to drive clean and ready for her *as she wanted it when she wanted it*. It was her due.

If there is anything that gets under the skin of the *real* people in Flyover regions, it is this all-too-common sense of entitlement expressed by the Hollywood set, performers and executives alike.

"Who Do They Think They Are?"

American egalitarianism—a prime value in Middle America—fights against this way of thinking and behaving with hammer and tongs. It brings immediate cries of "Who do they think they are?" and "How dare they! They put their pants on one leg at a time just like the rest of us!"

A close friend of mine was head of the art department for decades at one of the major Hollywood studios. In that capacity, he oversaw set design and construction and, on occasion, other studio construction.

A very successful and long-running TV show was shot on the studio lot, and—in a concession to the producers and stars of the show—the studio agreed to build more permanent quarters for the cast. Typically, the cast of such shows is housed in "trailers" which are pulled onto the lot. I put the word "trailers" in quotes, because these are like nothing you've seen at your local mobile home park. These are absolutely luxurious.

As a side bar, in 1979, actor Lyle Waggoner, the tall handsome guy on the *Carol Burnett Show,* started a company called Star Waggons to provide custom-fitted mobile residences for actors to live in while on location. These buggies may have spas, workout rooms, high-end sound, film, and TV equipment, or makeup stations in addition to the usual plush air conditioning and designer decorating amenities. For fun, visit <www.starwaggons. com> and see what I am talking about. I explain this to make it clear that the cast members of the successful TV shows were not suffering in makeshift hovels before the demand was presented for "permanent" housing on the studio lot.

My friend, the art department boss, designed lovely temporary apartments with standard eight-foot ceilings, and construction was about to begin on them when a problem arose. It seems that a female star on the show insisted that her apartment have a chandelier in the center of the living space. While this may not seem like such a big deal, it meant that the entire construction of that woman's apartment would have to be re-engineered to permit higher ceilings. Eight-foot ceilings wouldn't accommodate a chandelier of the type she demanded.

Flyover Reality Therapy

In the go-around between the producer and my friend, the matter escalated to the point that the producer said the star was threatening to quit the show if she didn't get her chandelier—whatever the cost and hassle to the studio. She was *entitled* to have her way. She was special.

The man-from-the-Red-States head of the art department told the producer, "I have a solution. Just say 'no' to her." He reasoned that the woman might fume and sputter, but that she wouldn't quit over a chandelier. Of course, if she had tried to quit, her agent and manager and everyone else getting golden eggs from her goose would have given the woman an "attitude adjustment." The producer did finally say "no." The star threw her tantrum, but showed up the next day for work.

This is one of thousands of stories like this. A very successful TV producer friend told me of one of the stars of a long-running network TV western who was getting too big for his cowboy britches, as the show entered the next ratings-busting season. As series get renewed and the network is making more and more money from sponsorship and rerun syndication, everybody who's part of the production demands more money. It's as sure as death and taxes in Hollywood. The producers of the show knew that this actor and his agent were prepared to "shoot the moon" in their contract demands for the next season.

Rising EQ

The cowboy actor's EQ, "Entitlement Quotient," had to be corralled (pun intended). It was already way out of control. Deciding to make a preemptive strike on the situation, the producers made two calls, one to the studio's central casting division and the other to the wardrobe department. When the actor and his agent later walked into the room to negotiate the upcoming season's contract, they were stunned to find half a dozen look-alike performers all in costumes like the actor typically wore on the show. The message was clear. The negotiations went rather well, with the injection of an "entitlement retardant" into the mix.

In a similar story told to me by the same TV producer, the star of a hit show was getting the idea that since he was so central to the long-running series' success, he could step beyond the bounds of the actor role and make decisions normally reserved for the director and producer of the show. No need to say that this didn't play well with the director and producer.

On the first read-through of the script for the next week's show—the first step in prepping a new episode—the actor became more and more subdued as he read that his character had become gravely ill. His character was taken to the hospital, given a diagnosis that he was terminal, and died. Every actor knows what it means when your character dies. You are in the unemployment line.

Noting from the demeanor of the arrogant actor that he had gotten the message, the producer said, "I tell you what. Let's not do this story this week. Let's hold it for the future. Hand me that other script." In the other script, the star's character was fine. But Mr. Bigstar knew from then on that he could be written out of the series in one episode. This was a restraint on his entitlement motivation.

The "Gimmie" Factor

Most people don't realize a number of things that go on in Hollywood and New York where celebrities are involved. The near-worship of celebrities by the masses elevates them to a position in which they come to believe that they are *owed* whatever they want. It becomes gimmie, gimmie, gimmie.

It is not at all uncommon for a big celebrity to take friends to an expensive restaurant and expect to have the restaurant "comp" the tab, however large it is. The thinking is that a star's appearance at the establishment is, or will be, such a boon to business that the restaurant owner will joyfully write off the tab as a cost of promoting his business.

This sense of entitlement for literal free lunches is fed by the fact that big stars actually get paid to show up at public venues, even for short visits. A Madison Avenue advertising veteran told me of a major public relations launch he was doing in Hollywood for a client's new product line. They wanted the event to grab headlines and knew that, for that to happen, they'd have to have some big stars attend it.

A novice to "the way things work" in this situation, my friend told me how he learned you get that to happen. You work through the big stars' agents to see if you can get them to attend the event, even for an hour. If the celebs agree, you negotiate a fee for their appearance. Depending on the current star power of the celebrity, this number could range from $10,000 to $25,000. After you secure two or more contracts for big names to appear, you begin to spread the buzz that they will be attending the event . . . and the press will be there. Two key factors here—big stars and the press.

As the well-sowed rumor circulates that Mr. Big Star and Ms. Bombshell will be attending the event (and the press will be there), it becomes easy to get other celebrities to attend. In Hollywood and New York, it is *de rigueur* to be at events where the top stars are in attendance, and did I mention the press will be there?

No one has ever paid me a five-figure sum just to show up at an event, but I suppose, if it were a common practice in my life, I might actually come to expect it. I might begin to feel *entitled* to the payment. Basically, I don't get the whole idea. It smacks of runaway narcissism to me. The millions of folks out there working for a living who don't get paid to show up at any venue but their work place don't get it either. It is repulsive to them to think that anybody could come to *expect* this kind of treatment.

"The Worst Time of My Year"

Years ago, I developed a friendship with the head of the Academy of Television Arts and Sciences. This is the organization which sponsors the Emmy awards honoring those who excel in various areas of the TV business. The annual Emmy awards are, as you know, one of the two biggest award nights of the year along with the Oscar awards given by the Academy of Motion Picture Arts and Sciences.

My friend and I were having lunch and I asked how things were going. He said, "I hate this time of year right before the award show." When I asked why, he explained it very clearly. You see, seating at the awards ceremony is something the academy controls, and the demand for prime seats is all-out war. I asked if it was for the best seats front and center. Much more complicated than that, he informed me.

Invitees demanded—not requested, but *demanded*—certain seats. It was a lot more than just the location of the seats. It was whether the seats were in areas where they would be viewed by the TV cameras covering the event. It was a question of who was sitting in front, behind, and beside them. It was also a question of the "seat fillers." The academy hires attractive people in formal dress who are "nobodies" to fill the empty seats of those celebs who step back stage to present awards. No self-respecting person would want to be seen on national television sitting next to a nobody, now would they? Then, too, nobody wants to be seated next to someone in the industry whom they loathe. Get the picture?

"You'll Never Work in This Town Again"

Assigning the seats based on academy criteria—not just the personal whims of the attendees—was a sufficient enough challenge. But dealing with those who were given seats they, for whatever reason, did not want made the task a nightmare. There were threats. There were pledges to get even. There were promises to call higher powers at the academy to get what they wanted. There were boastful threats comparable to the famous Hollywood line, "You'll never work in this town again." People screamed and yelled and demanded to talk to the person in charge. It was hell.

And just why was it that what could have been a simple matter of allocating tickets was an annual nightmare? The answer was clear. Many people felt *entitled* to get exactly what they wanted. Damnation to all the others who wanted tickets or who were more central to the purpose for the academy event. The entitlement culture was showing its ugly side.

To put this Hollywood conduct in perspective, can you imagine People in the "I" States behaving like this? Can you imagine this sort of nightmare for the annual Rotary Club Celebrity Dinner in Omaha, or even for tickets to the state high school basketball championship game in Indianapolis? It wouldn't happen.

Just Like Middle School . . . on Steroids

A professional musician friend in Hollywood, a guy who creates music for movies, has a very apt description of this entitlement culture. He says, "Hollywood is just like your junior high or middle school." Remember how it was? Being in the "in group" was life itself; not being included was death. There was obsession with what other kids thought. Wearing fashions and styles that were really cool was paramount. You didn't even want to be seen in the older family station wagon, so you had Mom drop you off a block from the school. Driven by adolescent insecurity, those of us in the seventh, eighth, and ninth grades were not only on thin ice socially, we were vulnerable psychologically and spiritually. Those days were precarious and, in many ways, miserable. So it is with Hollywood.

The first successful actor I met in the industry in the early eighties was a star in the popular comedy TV series *F Troop*. He expressed this insecurity to me in this way. "There's something sick about us actors, something missing. Most people are satisfied with the affirmation of family, friends, and a few professional peers, but not us. We are desperate to have our name in lights, to walk the red carpet, to get the standing ovation. When that happens, it is an incredible high, and we are on top of the world. But when the curtain falls, we are as miserable as we were before. It doesn't last." It's a little like being junior high homecoming king or queen on the weekend, and then going to school the next Monday and, once again, having to deal with the gossipy classmates and fight for recognition with the "big people" on campus.

Evidence of the "downer" Hollywood performers go through when the spotlight is no longer on them is revealed by tracking what happens to major stars when, suddenly, they are no longer in the limelight. Many of them self-destruct, get into substance abuse, become clinically depressed, and even attempt suicide. Their worth as persons is often so tied to the fickle flow of phony adulation from the industry and from their "fans" that not having that constant adrenaline rush of hero-worship sucks their psyches dry. It is little wonder that when fleeting celebrity status is with them, they feel *entitled* to keep it. To lose it is a fate worse than death.

"Show Me the Money"

The industry is cruel. The common expression, "You are only as good as your last movie" is another way of saying, "If you are not on top, you are worthless to us." This is a killer dynamic, because only about two percent of actors are on top at any given point in time . . . and that time is short.

A number of years ago, I did research on the employment status of members of the Screen Actors Guild (SAG). Only two percent made more than $200,000 acting in the previous year. Only six percent made $50,000. The rest of what was then about 120,000 SAG members obviously made less than fifty grand, and a third of them didn't earn a dime acting that year. Half of SAG members hadn't earned a nickel acting in three years. If 94 percent of SAG members earn less than $50,000 year—and most of them nothing approaching a living wage—it explains why there are lot of people in New York and Los Angeles waiting tables and selling real estate with excellent elocution! Let's face it, you don't live very well in New York or L.A. on fifty grand or less a year.

When I first came into the industry, I was mystified by the comment, "He's a *working* actor." How silly, I thought. If he were an electrician, you wouldn't say "He's a *working* electrician." Now, I understand the phrase. It means the actor is one of the three or four percent in the profession who can actually *make something approximating a living by acting*. Most can't.

Occupational Outlook Handbook, 2012 Edition, U.S. Bureau of Labor Statistics, indicates that, of the approximately 80,000 SAG members, only about 50 fall into the "highly paid" category with the median hourly wage at $20.26![1] Producers and Directors didn't do much better, just $34.31 an hour.[2] I just paid a plumber $110 an hour!

The distilled essence of this message is that if one is hoping to get rich, moving to Hollywood and New York for a job in entertainment is not the route to go. If a media professional feels *entitled* to make a lot of money for his craft, he is going to spend a lot of time depressed.

"When You're Hot, You're Hot. When You're Not, You're Not."

Not only is the pay lousy for the vast majority of people in show biz', any fame that comes to the handful is fleeting. For the rest, fame never comes. I hosted a television talk show that was syndicated across Canada in the late seventies. When my Phil-Donahue-type show was launched, an executive at Glen-Warren studio in Toronto told me, "We have the power to make you a household name in six weeks." While my show's success didn't give me name recognition even in any *neighborhoods*—to say nothing of in *every household*—the stated power of the medium gave me pause. Certainly, *American Idol* demonstrates this power.

If national name recognition can be achieved in six weeks, it is also true that national oblivion begins in thirty days. An Oscar-nominated actor told me that if you don't have some kind of visibility every thirty days, you are pretty much forgotten in a few months. Out of sight, out of mind. This explains why actors do talk shows, publicity stunts, lame celebrity game shows—*Hollywood Squares* comes to mind—and make sure they show up at any event at which there is a red carpet, the press, or the paparazzi.

I came out of a meeting at ABC when its offices were in Century City to discover a movie premier in progress. It was a standard Hollywood film launch—red carpet, paparazzi, string of limos, etc. I studied the dynamics of the event and decided that there was a very effective way to calculate the current celebrity status of those stepping onto the red carpets from the limousines. I call it the "flash effect."

As soon as a really big star hit the carpet, there was a cacophony of calls from the photogs to "Look here! Over here! Pose for us! Show us some leg!" The number of flashes were incalculable. When a not-so-hot person emerged from a limo, there would be few, if any, calls and only a few flashes. Every celebrity knew his status instantly by this "flash factor." The hurtful thing to me was to see some get scant recognition, even though it might not have been *five years* since they would have been the *center* of all the attention. What a short span of time between "star" and "has-been."

In the industry, the life cycle of an actor, one I'll name Joe Doaks, is described as follows :

> "Who's Joe Doaks?"
> "Joe Doaks is available."
> "Any chance of getting Joe Doaks?"
> "I wish we could afford Joe Doaks."
> "What we need is young Joe Doaks."
> "Who's Joe Doaks?"

Pretty sad commentary, really. Hardly the kind of track on which you'd like to be running for a fulfilling life and vocation, especially if you think you are destined to be a star.

Insecurity's Link to Entitlement

I was talking with the producer of a number of hit network comedy shows, and he expressed how eager he was for the show's upcoming summer hiatus to begin. I asked him if this was because of the killer production schedule and the grueling pace of week-to-week show creation. "No, it's working with *actors!* Do you have any idea what that's like?" Of course, I didn't.

> They're temperamental and whiny. They are 'hurt' if another actor gets more lines in the show than they do, or if they feel upstaged. You are constantly dealing with this immature behavior. Child actors are the worst, because you also have to deal with their demanding, overprotective parents. A producer friend of mine has a sign hanging in his office that says, 'REMEMBER, AN *ACTOR* KILLED ABE LINCOLN.'

Why are so many in the industry insecure? First, I think it is because *most are desperately insecure from childhood.* Most, like my *F Troop* friend, are running low in their affirmation reservoirs before they ever get to Hollywood. Many did not get sufficient love and affirmation from parents and others as children, and many were abused. As I noted before, childhood trauma is the single most determinant factor in celebrity narcissism according to celebrity psychiatrist Dr. Drew Pinsky.[3] It is the applause— delivered in more ways than just hand-clapping— that keeps them at some point of psychological equilibrium.

Emotionally fragmented people achieve in order to *be somebody*. *Emotionally whole* people achieve because *they know they are some-body*. Big difference. Entertainment has a lot of people who entered their profession because they were desperate to *be somebody*.

Second, show business people tend to **live lives driven by unre-alistic expectations.** They typically arrive in Hollywood or New York expecting to be a big star, to sell a screenplay and have it produced into a blockbuster movie, to win an Oscar or an Emmy . . . more than once, to become a household name . . . worldwide, to marry another rich and famous person, to command millions for their work, to live like a king or queen, etc. These vain hopes, in and of themselves, set media professionals up for misery. I explain this concept by a formula:

S = E/R.

<u>S</u>atisfaction in life is the result of <u>E</u>xpectations over <u>R</u>eality

Some corollaries to this formula are . . .

- If we live life with wildly unrealistic expectations, it enhances the probability that our lives will be unsatisfying.
- There are usually limits to what we can do to change the reality we experience in life, the "cards we are dealt."
- Adjusting expectations to a level more in keeping with reality enhances the potential for life satisfaction.

Third, **unrealistic expectations feed a sense of entitlement.** If my psychological image of myself is one who is superior to others—a "star"—I will deport myself as one. This is true even if I really am a wan-nabe, has-been, or never-was-gonna-be. This "terminal self-image fan-tasy" causes people to act in a way that is totally out of touch with the reality of who they are. They begin to act in a manner my father would have described as "I'd like to buy him for what he's worth and sell him for what he *thinks* he's worth." The world owes them . . . everything, they think.

Fourth, **the industry feeds both insecurity and a sense of entitle-ment.** Las Vegas draws millions to the city with the lure of "getting rich quick." Hollywood and New York show business draws hundreds of thousands with the lure of "getting famous quick." Hollywood is the Las Vegas of fantasy fame. The famous men's pickup line is, "I'll make you a star." It works. The extrapolation of that line is, "After this picture, you can name your price/buy the mansion in Malibu/be famous around the world." With even a modicum of success—as with one hugely successful movie or TV series—producers and directors, as well as performers, often go nuts. They act out their newfound, but fleeting, success, success to which they now feel entitled.

When your ship comes in, you know it won't be in the port long . . . so you'd better enjoy your shore leave to the max.

Meanwhile, Back at the Ranch

In those vast areas of America occupying the space between the Klieg lights of Sunset Strip and Times Square, there are the people Barack Obama condescendingly described as ". . . bitter, they cling to guns or religion or antipathy to people who aren't like them . . .."[4] Or, maybe not.

They live in worlds far removed from Hollywood, New York, and, for that matter, Washington. But they live in a world that does not feed exaggerated expectations of fame and fortune, doesn't seduce the populace with false notions that they are better than everybody else, and doesn't fawn over local celebrities and let them think that the rules don't apply to them. And, yes—on this point President Obama was accurate—they do cling to their faith in God. They believe that doing so will enable them to be fulfilled without great wealth, secure without great achievement, keep their families intact without therapy or rehab, provide transcendent meaning to the mundane, and provide a tranquility in their souls that Tinseltown doesn't possess and can't provide.

This spiritual "centering" and security among mature members of the Faith Community is a product of their deeply held belief that they are special creations of a loving God, a God who loves them and who loves them enough to sacrifice Himself for them. Their self-worth, then, derives from their conviction of immense transcendent value largely or totally separate from their personal performance. They do not achieve in order to become somebody special, they achieve because of the confidence they possess that they *are* somebody special and owe everything to the One who made them special.

By and large, these people don't feel *entitled*. They feel *grateful*. They are grateful for God's many good gifts, for His guidance and moral compass, and for simple things like love, family, health, friends, and community. They are grateful for America—seen as "super patriots" to the cynics—and don't want to see the bedrock virtues they believe made America the most successful and powerful nation ever undermined.

To some extent, God and His revealed pattern for successful living is at the center of life in Normalville.

THE FULCRUM

The God-and-Bible Factor

It Ain't Necessarily So . . .

As George and Ira Gershwin's 1935 folk opera *Porgy and Bess* unfolds, Sportin' Life, a drug dealer in the story, sings an irreverent song that became the show's second most popular with audiences—"It Ain't Necessarily So."[1] Selected stanzas from the song make its message clear:

> It ain't necessarily so
> The t'ings dat yo' li'ble
> To read in de Bible,
> It ain't necessarily so.
>
> Well, it ain't necessarily so
> Well, it ain't necessarily so
> Dey tells all you chillun
> De debble's a villun,
> But it ain't necessarily so!

To get into Hebben
Don' snap for a sebben!
Live clean! Don' have no fault!
Oh, I takes dat gospel
Whenever it's pos'ble,
But wid a grain of salt.[2]

Sure, the song was sung by an evil character in the show. Sure, the song's message was rebutted by another character, Serena, in her song, "Shame on All You Sinners!" Sure, it was "just entertainment." But, ironically, the issue addressed in this lighthearted song may well be the tipping point in the long-running conflict between Hollywood and Middle America's people of faith.

The pivotal Issue: Is the record of God and His relationships with humans found in the Hebrew Scriptures and the New Testament trustworthy or not? Is it really a true revelation from God of His ways and dealings with the race?

In the previous twelve chapters, I have laid out areas of conflict between people of faith in America and the dominant culture of the entertainment business. It should be clear, by now, that the "values distance" between the two camps is *light years*, and the crevasse between the two contingents is seemingly *insurmountable*. While that might be, I don't think the distance can be fully understood without analyzing the root causes.

The "Alternate God" Worshippers

When the God of Abraham, Isaac, and Jacob lays out His standards for successful living in the Torah, Exodus chapter twenty, He begins with the command, "You shall have no other gods before me" (Exodus 20:3). This foundational premise for the rest of the Decalogue is also basic to the life of faith. It becomes, at the outset of this discussion, the dividing line between those who predominate in media and those who typify the masses of the Moral Middle in America. Belief in God and basic trust in the main teachings of the Bible are central and pivotal to the value system of the Flyovers. This clearly is not the case for the primary movers and shakers in the world of entertainment.

When columnist and author Ann Coulter wrote her book dividing political conservatives from political liberals on the matter of faith, she titled the book, *Godless: The Church of Liberalism*.[3] Technically, Ann was wrong in her designation of the non-devout left as "godless." In reality, those who do not pursue a respectful relationship with the One whom Jews, Christians, and some Muslims view as "the true and living God" do, indeed, worship a god or multiple gods. As they serve these "alternate gods," they become guilty of violating Commandment Number One, the command not to elevate any other deity over the Giver of the Torah.

The fundamental dynamic pulling all mortals away from worshipping God is ego. Someone has suggested that the E, G, and O of the word stand for "Edging God Out." The opposite is I, G, I—Inviting God In. Surrendering to God is an uncomfortable and rather rare act of humility which flows violently at crosscurrents to our basic human nature. Some would claim that surrendering ego to God is actually impossible without divine assistance!

The "Self-Made" Person

God is an immovable object which stands in the way of our irresistible human drive to exalt ourselves, serve other deities of our own choosing, or promote ourselves to godlike status in the grand scheme of things. There is a sense in which every failure to recognize God's role in creation, provision, direction, and enrichment of life is a redirection of our innate need to worship a higher power away from the True Source of those good things.

First Century Jewish Rabbi Saul of Tarsus—AKA the Apostle Paul—writing in one of his letters to believers in Rome, weighed in on this point. He observed that the starting point for cosmic human guilt is (1) failure to honor and exalt God and (2) failure to express thanks for the good things He lavishly provides for His creatures (Romans 1:21).

The so-called "self-made man" is guilty of making a god of himself and shoving out any role that a benevolent creator-God might have had in (1) creating the conditions, (2) providing the intelligence or talent, or (3) arranging the opportunities for that person to have a life with multiple benefits. Some wag has suggested that you can always tell the "self-made person" . . . by the defects in workmanship!

Creating a life which operates on a day-to-day basis without deference to God is practical atheism—ordering one's life as if He does not exist. By this definition, a person may even go through the motions of religious observance and still be a practical atheist in daily life and decisions.

The Roots of the Difference

Over three decades working inside the entertainment industry, I have often asked myself, "What would have to change to get the leaders of the industry and American people of faith on the same page in worldview and values? I have concluded that change in two—just two—convictions would bring the two galaxies together more than any other.

Conviction No. 1: God must be the center of everything, and we must honor Him in all we do.

Conviction No. 2: The sacred Scriptures, the Bible, must be our guide for everything we think and do.

"Now, waaaiiit a minute," you say. "You've noted conflict over who's worthless and who's not, over the nature of media influence and accountability for what's produced and distributed, conflict over the nature of good and evil, God and faith, Jesus and being born again, over moral and political liberalism, over excess, and even over the definition of what is rational. You even included differences over Darwinism, origins, abortion, and homosexuality! There is no way that a change in two religious notions is going to weld that complex of massive breaks."

That would be a very reasonable observation, if change in those two convictions were mere alteration of "religious notions." They are not. Those two convictions hold the master key to a radical and revolutionary alteration in worldview, life, practice, and values.

Hollywood Bad Boy

Listen to this from one of Hollywood's most successful screenwriters:[4]

Why did God save the life of a man who had trashed, lampooned, and marginalized Him most of his life? Why did He take the time and the trouble to save me? It certainly wasn't because I had written *Basic Instinct* and *Showgirls*, right? Was it because my wife and I had four little boys we were trying to raise? Possibly.

Or was it God's divinely impish sense of humor? 'Who, you? You're praying? After everything you've done to break my commandments and after every nasty, unfunny thing you've written about Me and those who follow Me — now you're sobbing? Praying? Asking Me to help you? Hah! Okay, fine, I'll help you. But if I do, know this: My help will obliterate the old, infamous you. You'll wind up turning your life inside-out. You'll wind up stopping all of your excesses. You know what will happen to you? You'll wind up telling the world what I did for you. You'll wind up carrying My cross in church. Yes, I make all things new—and you will be new, too.'

Joe Eszterhas had the world on a string in Hollywood. Movies he has written have brought in more than one billion dollars at the box office.[5] He lived up to his personal description in the above two paragraphs. By his own admission, he was a hard living, chain-smoking, womanizing, substance-abusing guy with no time for any "Flyover values." His obscenity-and-nudity-filled movies provide stark evidence of that.

Joe embraced Conviction Number One. He asked God into his life and made Him center of everything. He decided to honor Him.

Hear his words again:[6]

Seven years ago, I sat down on a curb near my home, sobbing, and asked God to help me. I had just had surgery for throat cancer. I still had a trache in my throat. I had been told that if I didn't stop smoking and drinking immediately, I'd die. I desperately didn't want to die. I adored my wife and children. But I knew I couldn't stop. I'd started smoking when I was twelve and drinking when I was fourteen. I was now fifty-seven years old.

I cried and begged God to help me . . . and He did. I hadn't prayed since I was a boy. I had made fun of God and those who loved God in my writings. And now, through my sobs, I heard myself asking God to help me . . . and from the moment I asked, He did.

What Joe calls a "miracle," the strength to defeat his addictions, is matched by what his throat surgeon, Dr. Marshall Strome, calls another miracle. This is the doctor who removed eighty percent of Joe's larynx to get the cancer out. Dr. Strome told Joe that the throat tissue has regenerated so remarkably that a doctor examining his throat today wouldn't be able to tell that there was ever cancer there.

Joe's story is contained in his book, *Cross Bearer: A Memoir of Faith*.[7] You can read it for yourself. In a single act of contrition, Joe switched to Flyover thinking! Since then, carrying the cross in services at his church, Joe is beginning to live by Conviction Number Two. He is making the Scriptures his guide for everything he thinks and does.

"Give Me a Break!"

At this point, I can hear the cynics roar. "Give me a break! This is anecdotal! This is only one story. What does it have to do with anything?"

Right, it is just one story. But's let's think about this story a bit. It is true that a single incident does not (usually) a solid argument make. But a single story that can be replicated thousands . . . no, hundreds of thousands . . . no, *millions* of times over decades . . . no, centuries . . . no, *millennia* has got to be taken seriously.

If someone walks into the room with a fried egg hanging over his ear and claims, "This egg gives me peace and joy and happiness!" you can ridicule him. But, if you discover that there are millions of people from all eras of time, of all nationalities, of all socioeconomic and educational levels, and of all ages and genders who experience the identical "fried-egg-peace-and-joy phenomenon," you'd better check it out.

I personally know hundreds of media professionals who could tell the same story Joe Eszterhas has told of their own lives. Slightly different details, but the same basic story. Our organization has a data base of thousands of working professionals in film, TV, new media, and such who could tell the same story Joe tells of themselves. Imagine, thousands of people wearing fried eggs over their ears. Better check them out.

I know of the transforming power of faith in God and in His Son Jesus Christ. I can't speak for Judaism or other religions, but I have watched men and women for whom getting drunk and "hooking up" was what they lived for. I've seen them be changed so much that, six months later, they'd stopped partying and couldn't wait to get to a prayer meeting and Bible study. They said the radical change in values came by "giving themselves to God" or "Giving their lives to Jesus Christ." I don't know what constitutes "miracle change" for you, but that comes pretty close in my book!

Getting Religion. Big Deal.

"Fine," you say. "So, Joe Eszterhas (and a few hundred million others) had a dramatic change in his life and values by getting religion. Did I understand that you think this would also change his values about all those other issues . . . like abortion, accountability, liberalism, homosexuality, and rationality?" I do think that.

Let's take a journey through the list of divisive issues and see how embracing Conviction Number One and Conviction Number Two might change perspectives.

Let's start with **abortion**. This is a nice flash point for those in both ideological camps. If a person makes God central to life and makes the Scriptures the sole guide for life and conduct, the divine origin of human life becomes an immediate issue. If God creates a human soul in tandem with the linkage of a sperm and an egg—or even at the first breath—and if human life is a sacred treasure to be stewarded for its Creator, then deciding to abort becomes an entirely different issue. The POC, product of conception, becomes more than a benign collection of cells that can be ripped, sucked, crushed, or poisoned to termination with impunity. It becomes a matter of dealing with a divinely created human being, fashioned in the image of God, and possessing an eternal spirit.

Whoa! That makes a woman's "choice" radically heavier. It may even constitute a violation of Commandment Number Seven, the one about taking life.

On the other hand, if there is no Author of that tiny life inside the womb, and we are all just here as end products of cosmic chance and chemistry, abort away! The choice carries no accountability to anyone but yourself.

What about **entitlement?** With God at the center of life and His Book the guide, we learn that we came naked into the world, exit just as naked, and every good gift we receive comes from Him as an unde-served act of divine beneficence. As the Creator and Final Arbiter of all we are and have, He—not we—has the right to bless or withhold bless-ing as He chooses. We have no "rights" in the matter and are not "en-titled" to anything but His wrath except by His grace. In answer to the brash question, "Don't you know who I am?" the answer comes back, "I know very well who you are. You are a morally flawed creature whose own arrogance has blinded you to your shortcomings and caused you to assume you *deserve* My favor. You don't."

If, on the other hand, you are the sole master of your fate and the captain of your soul, you can establish your own level of entitlement and go for it!

What about **superiority?** The notion that one group or person is inherently superior to another is a major affront to the concept of equality which God reveals in the Scriptures. In a host of passages, the Book teaches that all humans stand equal before God. Thus, the flow of self-righteousness on both sides of the divide—not limited to the *religious* type—is hypocritical and without merit. The holier-than-thou of one side is just as baseless as the better-than-thou of the other. As it is often said in Christian circles, "The ground is level here at the foot of the cross." The social one-upsmanship we practice is sheer vanity.

What about **sex outside of marriage?** If one believes—as the Scriptures teach—that sex is a sacred rite of intimate union between a man and a woman in a lifelong covenant of fidelity, then the idea of "hooking up" with any person who will crawl into bed with us or, for that matter, one whom we merely "love," becomes a profane act. It demeans the divine purpose for the act, impairs the ultimate richness of sex when one does marry, and reduces it to selfish fulfillment rather than an act of giving to another in loving commitment.

On the other hand, if there is no God, and there is no "morality" attached to sexual behavior, it is as meaningless as scratching an itch. Scratch away!

What about **accountability** for the impact we have on others by our actions, media product, and such? The Scriptures would dictate that our obligation to our "neighbor" transcends even our own personal benefit. It is a matter of serious consideration if, in any way, we are guilty of harming another person. From the expansive teachings of the Torah to the bold teachings of Jesus, benevolent attitudes and beneficent acts toward others are a primary obligation. Exploitation of others for our own purposes is condemned clearly and repeatedly. Jesus went so far as to state that those who exploit others would be better off having a large millstone hung around their necks and to be drowned in the depths of the sea (Matthew 18:6). Living by this moral guideline would surely affect decisions about film content, destructive TV programming, or perverse internet stuff.

Without accountability to any galactic Moral Arbiter, throw any kind of horrific content at the public you wish, so long as it gets ratings, sells tickets, or makes you richer and more powerful.

What about **homosexuality and lesbianism?** If there is no God and, thus, no transcendent natural law or divine moral restraint on sexual behavior, then there is no basis for deciding that sex between partners in any category is "wrong." Right and wrong become irrelevant and merely arbitrary social conventions. No problem with same sex intimacy. No problem with adult sex with children or animals or, for that matter, inner tubes or garden rakes. If one wants to marry a man, woman, child, animal, or garden rake, we can dispense with notions of "immorality." A person should "be free to marry anyone/anything they love."

However, if God is the center of our lives and motivation (Conviction Number One) and Holy Writ has determinations about the morality of such behaviors (Conviction Number Two) then sexual practice becomes a very different matter. To claim that those who believe in and live by the Two Convictions "hate" people who don't live by them is a red herring. It doesn't matter whether those persons are loved or hated; it is a matter of the objective evil or good of their practices.

Interestingly, when people commit to Conviction Number One, it changes their *entire* life orientation, sexual and otherwise. Libertine men and scarlet women become chaste. Gays and lesbians live straight lives. Even child molesters repent and become honorable in their sexual attitudes and acts.

What about **language?** Wallowing in verbal filth and slandering God and sacred things tend to disappear from the speech of those who pursue Convictions Number One and Two. A very successful producer of big studio films said that the first notice her peers gave that something had changed after she gave her life to God was that they asked about her language. "You don't swear anymore, do you?" was the question. She admitted to "swearing like a sailor" before she gave her life to God through Jesus Christ.

A lot of the nonsense about PG, PG-13, and R ratings would be nonexistent if the standards of the Scriptures were adhered to by the TV "broadcast standards" people and film content gatekeepers:

> Finally, brothers and sisters, whatever is true, whatever is noble, whatever is right, whatever is pure, whatever is lovely, whatever is admirable—if anything is excellent or praiseworthy—think about such things (Philippians 4:8).

> Do not let any unwholesome talk come out of your mouths, but only what is helpful for building others up according to their needs, that it may benefit those who listen (Ephesians 4:29).

What about **excess?** The Scriptures have massive content on saving, being trustworthy stewards of resources, and investing wisely. Heaping excess on our own ego satisfaction and hogging the best of the best for ourselves in pursuit of our own narcissism isn't supported by the Faith. It's an evidence of selfish covetousness and greed.

What about **political ideology?** The Scriptures have significant content supporting private ownership of property, honorable payment of taxes, responsible dispatching of responsibility to the poor and disenfranchised, the evils of greed, the responsible exercise of political power, and the role of "masters" to *serve, not exploit*, those under their oversight. The principles of the Scriptures provided the conceptual basis for the U.S. Constitution, and our political system works well only when these principles are followed.

What about **origins** and **Darwinism?** Let's face it. Cosmology and the origin of the species are radically different subjects with God out of the picture. If there is no Creator, then we are left to come up with big bang, little bang, or other explanations for the cosmos. No deity was the precipitating cause of life (originally). No God worked to develop plant and animal forms (progressively). There is no transcendent reason for the uniqueness of humans from higher forms of primates (ultimately). There is no designer of the intricate and complex patterns we see through the microscope and the telescope (profoundly). With no higher power in the picture in any of these dimensions, then we are free to theorize at will. If, however, as the first verse in the Torah declares, "In the beginning *God created* the heavens and the earth . . .," all bets are off.

Trust me. I've witnessed this personally hundreds of times. Once people open up to God personally, their cosmology and perspective on "intelligent design" begin to change radically. Once there is a realization at the personal level that "chance factors" are trumped by God's divine will, the God Factor begins to trump every other area of their "probability" thinking.

I have no doubt that if an epidemic of Convictions One and Two broke out in film and television, there would be a lot of remakes of documentaries on the origins of the solar system and the missing links between humans and primates. The story lines would fit more nicely with the thinking of those from the Red States today. We know the basis for that thinking. The research our organization commissioned through

ARG revealed that 88 percent of active Christians believe in the literal interpretation of the Scriptures.[8]

"Surely, **rationality** is independent from your Two Convictions!" you say. "How can matters of *reason* be subject to religious commitments?"

If reason were unfettered by emotions and will, I would agree. But, I have found that much of what we determine to be "reasonable" should be described as "reasonable *to me*." Objective, arms-length fact, evidence, and logic have little to do with most of our "reasoning." It works this way.

> *What the **heart** truly loves, the **mind** creatively and cleverly embraces and justifies, and the **will** eventually executes.*

A good bit of human "reasoning" is really driven by *personal choice* that is intellectualized. We *choose* to believe and disbelieve a lot more things than we are compelled to believe or disbelieve by purely rational and evidential data. As a result, our reasoning is a lot more suspect than any of us realizes. The image we have of ourselves as reaching totally objective, facts-based decisions and conclusions is largely myth. We are fundamentally creatures of *will*, not rationality. Most of our decisions are reached because we *want* to make them.

The zinger in my "two conviction solution" is that most people don't *want* to submit to God nor make His revelation central to their lives. Reason has little to do with it. It's a matter of will.

Getting Religion. A Really Big Deal!

When Conviction Number One is implemented, and God is made the center of our lives through submission to Him, there is a kind of mental "nuclear blast" that takes place. Sometimes, as early as the next day, people who have opened their lives to God realize that they see things differently from before making Commitment Number One. With neither brainwashing, indoctrination, nor exposure to ideas they previously despised, they find themselves embracing them.

Having God and His revelation at the center of life is a complete game changer.

CHAPTER FOURTEEN

"WHAT? YOU'RE A DECENT HUMAN BEING?"

The Demise of Demonization

Part I: Accentuate the Positive

In the decades of mud-slinging between the Hollywood and faith community camps, it seems that all sight has been lost of the immense good coming out of both worlds. There is probably not a conservative Christian in America outside of the industry who fully recognizes the generous spirit of those who derive their livelihood from entertainment businesses.

I was in the lobby of the ABC television network years ago when it was in Century City. While waiting for my appointment, I noticed a small stack of brochures on a lamp table. They were for the Entertainment Industry Foundation (EIF). I was stunned by the overview it provided of the organization.

Founded in 1942 by Samuel Goldwyn with friends Humphrey Bogart, James Cagney, and the Warner brothers, EIF was established "on the belief that the entertainment industry was in a unique position to truly help others. Their vision was to unify Hollywood's generous giving in order to maximize the amount of charitable dollars raised annually, and to guarantee that worthy charities receive these contributions."[1]

Throughout its history, the Entertainment Industry Foundation has focused on some of the most pressing needs of our time: from the first grants directed to wartime agencies like the United States Organizations (USO) and American Red Cross, to providing funding and creating awareness to help eradicate childhood polio.

Today, EIF has grown to a $100 million charitable organization. Thanks to the commitment of an extraordinary number of people and companies, EIF is able to champion a wide variety of worthy causes. Annually, EIF funds more than 300 charitable organizations within the greater Los Angeles area and throughout the nation.

While people of faith might differ in the choice of a few of the charitable causes supported, it would be criminal to ignore the magnanimity of the industry's professionals.

Likewise, industry professionals, in their rush to marginalize those who are devout in their faith, overlook the immense contribution conservative Jews and Christians make to the planet.

Part II: The Power of Confession

Prince of DreamWorks

Jeffrey Katzenberg had a good plan. In 1998, four years into the new Hollywood studio named DreamWorks SKG, Jeffrey—the "K" in SKG— wanted to make a blockbuster animated biblical epic film. The story of Moses, the Hebrew patriarch who was rescued by Pharoah's daughter and raised in the courts of Egypt to lead Israel to the promised land, seemed to be a surefire winner. Titled, *Prince of Egypt*, the film had incredible upside potential.

Its potential lay in the fact that it is an incredibly compelling story, timeless and nearly universal in its appeal. If embraced by the major religions which trust the Hebrew Scriptures' account of Moses, it could have enormously broad appeal—even to people who are not typically moviegoers. Based on the success of *Ten Commandments* and other biblical epics, it could become a perennial favorite for decades to come.

The idea also had strong downside potential. In a story like this, you have to steer around the religious traditions and sensitivities of millions. If these details are not handled carefully and treated with care, they can cause an otherwise great movie to tank before the first theatrical release. Jeffrey knew all this.

Very wisely, he decided to bring a sampling of leaders from all segments of the religious world—Jewish rabbis from all branches of Judaism, Protestant and Catholic leaders from a variety of Christian denominations, orders, and structures, evangelicals, pentecostals, charismatics, and even some Muslim clerics—for counsel on the story. This was not just for show. DreamWorks paid many of the guests' expenses and brought them in early enough in the film's development that substantive changes could be made in the story and portrayals. Most impressively, Katzenberg and his team thoroughly listened, documented the recommendations, and followed the counsel they received. This was largely unprecedented.

Clergy Paranoia

The response among the more conservative ministers in the Christian community was suspicion. I got calls from friends across the nation asking if this was legit. Did DreamWorks really want their counsel? Was this just a marketing ploy? Was this a trap? Was this like the overtures execs at Universal Studios made in 1988 saying they wanted to screen *The Last Temptation of Christ* for Christian ministers, then used the courtship of the clergy to hold off the protest so they could capitalize on the furor at the box office?

I did my reconnaissance and sensed that—as unusual as the offer was for a Hollywood studio—it was legitimate. I recommended that the ministers accept the invitation and certainly was pleased to accept the one I received.

The group of clergy with which I attended was diverse. The presentation was incredibly earnest and thorough. The interaction was not with some low-level functionary at the studio. It was with Jeffrey Katzenberg himself and his number two person on the project. I was impressed, if for no other reason than by estimating the number of hours Jeffrey put into meeting with all these delegations of clergy. This, in an environment in which heads of studios take ten-minute pitch meetings. He really had to believe in the strategy.

I followed up that contact with a brief private interaction with Jeffrey. "Level with me," I asked him. "How were you treated by the evangelicals? Did they beat you up, or did it go okay?"

"It went extremely well," he replied, "In fact, I wish I had received as good a treatment from some of the other groups."

Then, he told me this story to seal his point. He said that a Christian minister "sitting in my office right where you're sitting" asked for his forgiveness. He confessed that when he came to DreamWorks at the studio's invitation, he had come with wrong attitudes. He suspected motives, was sure the invitation was some kind of a ploy, and came just to prove his suspicions. He confessed that he had been treated with respect and could see that the motivation to seek counsel was authentic. He admitted he was embarrassed for impugning the motives of Katzenberg and the other DreamWorks people. He was authentically regretful.

There has to be a lesson in that kind of responsible thinking and action.

The Power of Confession

It is clear to anyone with even a smattering of Judeo-Christian teaching that confession and forgiveness are keys to right living, healthy human relationships, and godliness. The Jewish faith observes Yom Kippur as a time to clear accounts with God and man. Christians teach forgiveness of others as a precondition for receiving God's forgiveness. Not necessarily so in the culture of Hollywood. It is clear to me that—on both sides of the Hollywood/Faith Community divide—both confession and forgiveness are conspicuous by their absence.

Just once, it would be refreshing to hear some Hollywood studio or network executive ask forgiveness of the Faith Community for the words or actions against them, their faith, or their God. It has happened, but it is all too rare. Typically, Tinseltown decision makers just go silent and do damage control when they or some of their people have done violence to people of faith. Worse, many just stonewall and pretend no offense ever occurred. Doing so communicates an arrogant, elitist attitude.

On the faith side, there is some confessing to do as well. The sins of the religious conservatives definitely need atonement. On this point, let me tell you of an experiment that a very devout Christian conducted, one which became the heart of a film with an intriguing name, *Lord, Save Us From Your Followers*.[1]

Dan Merchant decided to conduct "man on the street" interviews across America. To prompt the interviewees to respond at a deeper level, Dan wore a white jump suit plastered with bumper stickers and slogans of a wildly diverse nature. Some were pro-choice, some pro-life. There were messages on both sides of a lot of hot-button issues.

Intercepting people on the streets, Dan asked which of his jumpsuit messages expressed their viewpoints and why? The idea worked really well, and people were engaged almost immediately. He learned a lot from those interviews and began to form some pretty clear opinions from what people told him.

And He Wasn't Even Catholic

Then, Merchant got a crazy idea. He rented booth space at a gay and lesbian festival and erected a larger-than-real-life confessional booth such as one would find in a Catholic church. It was divided by a screen, and Dan sat in the seat of the priest.

As each person entered and sat on the confessional side of the booth, Dan would explain that this was a very different type of confession time. He indicated that *he* would be doing the confessing. The film footage was stunning. As Dan confessed wrong attitudes, bigotry, and unkindness to the gay or lesbian individuals in the booth, many didn't know how to handle it. He confessed not just his personal wrongs, but wrongs of the Christian community and of churches.

Accustomed to being on the receiving end of rejection and hostility, many recipients of his earnest and vocal repentance were stunned into, first, silence, then tears, then often tender expressions of sharing their hurts and gratitude for somebody's caring.

It seemed that an earnest expression of contrition was the nuclear power that atomized the walls of separation and generated a genuine spiritual connection between a very straight, very conservative Christian and some very gay, very liberal gays and lesbians. Funny how that happens. Could it be a divine principle?

Headline News

During the conflict between the Christian community and the leaders of Universal Studios in 1988 over the release of *The Last Temptation of Christ*, I got caught in the middle. A producer friend had asked me to join him in a consulting effort on the film with Universal execs Tom Pollock, Sid Sheinberg, and others. When it became clear that the honchos at Universal had no intention of editing out content such as the scene of Jesus having sex with Mary Magdalene, my associate and I joined the open opposition to the film's release.

During that time, I was getting information from inside the studio, some of which became part of news releases and statements to journalists. The religion editor for the *L.A. Times* at that time was a fine man named John Dart. John and I were in regular communication, as he sought to keep up with the building dynamics of a protest which eventually saw 25,000 people conduct a peaceful march outside Universal Studios—the largest protest in the history of film.

Then, one day in the midst of this turmoil and press warfare, I was chagrined to realize that I had wrongly attributed some very damning direct quotes about the Christian protesters to Universal Pictures Chairman Tom Pollock. The statements were hideous, and Tom was guiltless. The statements were made by another Universal employee. Embarrassed and guilty, I decided that the right thing to do was to write Tom a letter of apology. That I did and sent it off to him.

When John Dart and I conversed shortly thereafter, I confessed my embarrassing mistake and provided him with the wording in the apology. I thought little of it until the next day's *Times* hit my sidewalk. There it was, a big headline touting that I had apologized to Mr. Pollock for the wrongful attribution. A friend noted that it was a rare occurrence when an apology made headlines in the *L.A. Times*.

Whether or not this is true, I've wondered. Are honest apologies so rare that they fit the definition of "headline news" in Hollywood? If so, perhaps it is time to make more headlines like this. Maybe it would tear down some walls.

Years later, when Universal Studios had a change of ownership, I approached the new owner with what I thought was a good idea. I reminded him that multitudes had ill feelings toward the studio because of *Temptation*, and perhaps millions were still in some kind of boycott mood. I suggested a public apology for the previous owners' offense to millions of Christians and a declaration that the new owners would eschew such behavior. I suggested that it might get his new regime off to a good start to clear the air. He responded coldly, "We're not apologizing to anybody." I believe that decision was a huge mistake. Millions of offended believers would have warmed to Universal's new management. Apart from being the right thing to do, it wouldn't have been bad for business!

Maybe it's time for adversaries on both sides of the Hollywood/Faith Community divide to start making some apologies. Could it hurt? I believe that some of the most powerful words in the English language are these seven: "I was wrong. Will you forgive me?" Uttering them in honesty often starts something beautiful . . . like reconciliation.

They also go forward who go penitently backward.

Part III: Separating Issues from Persons

In 2012, I got word from a former ABC executive that the network was launching a TV pilot titled, *Good Christian Bitches*. The series was based on a book by the same name written by Kim Gatlin. It was produced by Darren Star of *Sex and the City* and *90210*. The story line involved a reformed "mean girl" who returns to her hometown of Dallas to find herself fodder for malicious gossip from women in the Christian community.[2] The fight was on . . . again.

Blogger Bryan Fischer called ABC's naming of the show a "hate crime" and suggests, not unfittingly, ". . . Imagine if the pilot were entitled *Good Muslim Bitches*, or *Good Jewish Bitches*, or *Good Black Bitches*. The outrage would be deafening."[3] Fischer reminds his readers that President Obama pronounced that "It would be wrong to 'demonize' Muslims" and calls on him to stop ABC's demonizing of the Christian community. He wants U.S. Attorney General Eric Holder to pursue action against the network for committing a hate crime.[4]

So, typically, the conflict was handled poorly by both sides, as is commonly the case. Bob Iger, head of Disney ABC, was personally castigated by the more raucous voices in the Faith Community. It got personal. ABC execs, to their credit—avoided publicly denouncing the "lunatic fringe" of the Religious Community and citing the First Amendment. They changed the name of the show to "Good Christian Belles," and, finally, to "GCB" to make the title a little bit less "in your face." The show faded into oblivion like most cancelled TV series. But the offense will remain for a long time.

The point for both sides to hear is that, whatever else happens, the issues must be separated from the persons. In counseling, I've found that some people are utterly incapable of doing this. Let me explain by defining the behaviors of the "mergers" and the "separators."

The Mergers

Those who cannot separate issues from persons I call "mergers." They are marked by the following behaviors:

- If you differ with them on issues, they take it personally.
- They tie the relationship directly to shared viewpoints.
- Their agreement with you on issues determines their feelings toward you both positively and negatively (agree=warm; disagree=cold).
- Intellectual disagreement is viewed as interpersonal conflict.

The Separators

The "separators" are those who find it easy to separate issues from persons. They typically possess the following attributes:

- They see no link between a quality relationship and agreement on issues.
- It never occurs to them that disagreeing on an issue might threaten the friendship.
- They can vigorously defend a contrary viewpoint and, at the same time, strongly communicate love and caring.
- By separating the intellectual dimension from the feelings dimension they can interact at a deep and passionate level without taking any of the interaction personally.

In application, *people of devout faith* who are separators could interact with media leaders assuming positive motivation until proven otherwise. They could explain themselves without rancor, defend their positions without accusation, and retain the focus on differences of viewpoint without making the interchange personal or making personal attacks. They would be able to listen and ask questions as well as declare and denounce.

In application, *media decision makers* who are separators would be able to listen to the expressions of people of faith without prejudging them, marginalizing them, or dismissing out of hand their concerns and positions. They could respond to the passion of the people of faith without becoming personally defensive and retributive.

Could We Bottle This?

Surrounding the release of *The Passion of the Christ* movie in 2004, I established a very deep, trust relationship with an Orthodox Jewish rabbi. As the relationship deepened, we came to discover so much in common and so many things we admire and appreciate about each other.

One New Year's Eve day, he called to wish me a happy new year, and expressed appreciation for our friendship. He said, "I just wish we could bottle what we have and send it to the Palestinians and the Israelis."

I responded, "You know what we have is love. I may be more comfortable expressing it than you, but I love you, and I know you love me."

"Yes, but considering the fundamental differences in the way we believe . . . ."

"Look, I've been married for 48 years, and my wife and I have had some *fundamental differences* in the way we've believed. But, they haven't kept us from loving each other!"

In the final analysis, what Hollywood and the people of faith need more than anything else is some determined good will toward each other. It may take a while to get to the level of "love," but doesn't every loving relationship start with good will and an acquaintanceship?

In my organization's Corporate Seminar, we suggest ways for media executives to relate more effectively to people of faith. One suggestion is "get to know a conservative Christian on your peer level socially." Most people in media don't have a single social relationship with a person of deep Christian faith. Conversely, most of the people of faith don't know any media gatekeeper from either Hollywood or New York personally. They typically know few nonbelievers well.

This is the perfect setup for the demonization that is very common between the two constituencies. One of my associates says, "Distance demonizes." While ill will is the primary spark of demonization, distance surely makes it easier to fuel the fire.

Part IV: Seeking Divine Guidance

"They Actually *Prayed*!"

In 2004, the organization I head, Mastermedia International, came up with an idea which we launched that year. The concept was to host a very classy prayer breakfast in the heart of Hollywood and call Christian believers and other people of faith from across the nation to come to Filmland to pray for the leaders in media. Since 1986, we had been mobilizing prayer among tens of thousands of believers through the *Media Leader Prayer Calendar,* a listing of one or two power brokers and influencers per day. The prayer breakfast, we thought, needed to be different.

We asked ourselves, "Hollywood's overseers have seen all kinds of angry people come onto their turf to protest, complain, attack, and boycott. Have they ever had hundreds come to town to *pray* for them? Might it be a good thing to do?"

On October 1, 2004, about 500 people paid $125 a ticket at the Beverly Hilton for an event that—unlike a lot of so-called prayer breakfasts—didn't feature a talk or politicians. It featured *prayer*. It was endorsed by a number of prominent people in media and opened by *Purpose Driven Life* author, Rick Warren. It featured John Tesh, singers from The Fifth Dimension, film legend Rhonda Fleming, then Charter Communications head Carl Vogel, and music icon Pat Boone.

The press release expressed the sentiment behind the event:

> 'The message to Hollywood's elite is that there are millions of Christians who care enough about them to pray for them, not just boycott, protest, or bash them,' says breakfast founder Dr. Larry Poland. 'We want to send media leaders a positive message of love and forgiveness.'

Attendees prayed! Five prominent media professionals led the guests in prayer. Each guest had a list of five of the top 365 most powerful and influential media leaders on a place card. Individually, they prayed for them.

A professed atheist studio executive who attended was blown away. "We need to have one of these in every city!" was his response. A Jewish rabbi who attended a breakfast said, "I have never felt the presence of God so strongly as I did that morning."

Variety columnist, Brian Lowry, wrote that the prayer breakfast "reveals a little-seen side of Christianity" and "showcased a side of the Christian community that receives scant exposure compared with their sexier (by media standards, anyway) hellfire-breathing brethren." He went on, "And given the polls indicating a vast majority of Americans consider themselves pious, Hollywood ignores the portion it can reason with at its peril—commercially, if not ecumenically."[4]

Prayer Changes People

An old maxim often hanging on the walls of believers' homes declares, "Prayer Changes Things." More accurately, prayer changes US! Could it hurt to have media professionals and the people of faith across the nation come together and pray . . . for reconciliation, for the building of trust, for the cessation of hostilities, for the tearing down of walls?

In a five-minute talk at the breakfast I took my own medicine and expressed the following apology:

> If God is a forgiving God, we all need to buy into that forgiveness through repentance. I ask forgiveness of any non-Christian in this room who has been demeaned or shunned or assaulted by one of us. To any Jewish person—I say on behalf of all of us—forgive us for not giving you the love and respect our very Jewish Savior would ask us to show you. To every gay or lesbian person in this room who has been pummeled by one of us in the illusion that our sins are on a lesser order of magnitude than your sins, please forgive us. The ground is level here at the foot of the cross, and we all need His redemption.

In the four annual breakfasts we held before the economy shut them down, those words of apology drew the most positive reaction from guests and in the press. While it's humbling to admit our faults, it is redemptive and refreshing to hear repentant words expressed to us.

What would happen if an epidemic of "repentancitis" would break out and go viral? I believe the warfare between Hollywood and people of faith would begin to subside.

Part V: Taking the First Step

Domestic Nonviolence

Years ago, my wife and I had a serious argument over some relatively insignificant issue I don't even remember. But, hey, we aren't violent people. We didn't throw pots or pans, scream or yell, or engage in profane discourse. We just sat in two matching gold chairs in our living room for about an hour and in normal tones of voice said unkind things to each other.

In time, the old clock on the wall finally said it was time to turn in, so we did. Believe me, it's no thrill getting into bed with someone with whom you are having a fight. But, fortunately, we have a big bed. So, I clung to my side of the bed, and she held to the brink on her side.

Then, it happened. I began hearing this little voice in my mind. You know what I mean. It was not like one of the voices psychotic people hear, it was the "still, small voice" of my conscience. Probably even the voice of God.

"You said some pretty unkind things to her," was the first message.

"Did you hear what she said to me?" was my retort.

"Yes, but you are responsible for *your* words, not hers." I argued with what I have come to recognize as the Voice of God in my inner person—an exercise in futility, to be sure. I lost the argument, as I always do.

Finally, I said in my heart, "Well, okay, I'll meet her half way."

"No, no 'half way' stuff. I want you to exercise spiritual leadership in this. I want you to confess 100 percent of your part. Her part is not your business."

I got that sick feeling in the pit of my stomach like you get when you know you've just been caught with your hand in the cookie jar. In my spirit, I said, "Uncle! I'll make it right with her."

I hate those miserable moments when you know you have to surrender, eat dirt, 'fess up, ask forgiveness. Miserable.

I finally broke the deafening silence of our bedroom with a few hesitant words. "Honey?" No response. "I'm sorry. I said some really unkind things to you. I've asked God to forgive me. Will you forgive me?" Silence for what seemed like an eternity.

Then, I heard noises like maybe she was starting to cry, and she burst forth with, "It wasn't all your fault!" It was now like sobbing.

A strange thing happened. The great gulf between the two distant sides of our bed was suddenly bridged. We embraced, and our hearts started healing. The reconciliation didn't begin until one of us took that first conciliatory step.

A Veritable Revolution

Isn't there a lesson here? What might it be like if every strident televangelist began contacting heads of networks and studios to ask forgiveness for slanderous words and vicious verbiage used against them?

It might go like this in a letter to Mr. or Ms. Biggie at XYZ studio:

> Dear Chairperson,
>
> On my weekly TV show/in a recent blog/in last week's sermon, I tore into you and your company verbally and publicly and, in so doing, showed lack of respect for and unkindness to you. The behavior was not consistent with my professed faith and ethics. I recognize that this was the wrong thing to do, and I ask you to forgive me.
>
> I would love to sit down for lunch sometime to express my regrets in person.
>
> Cordially,
>
> Rev. Joe Johnson

If such were to happen, every ER unit within miles of Hollywood and New York media centers would be flooded with network and studio executives, producers, directors, and trade magazine journalists suffering from cardiac arrest.

On the other side, what kind of shock would spread among the Faith Community, if, suddenly, heads of networks and studios, writers and producers and performers began apologizing for attacking the faith, the leadership, or the sacred icons of people of faith?

It might go something like this in an ad in the *New York Times* and *L. A. Times:*

To people of faith:

As head of XYZ Network/ MNO studio/*Variety* magazine, I have come to realize that spokespersons for our company and product which we have produced have mocked your Christian/Jewish faith, shown disrespect for your God, and have slandered your spiritual leaders.

In a decision of our Board of Directors, it was determined that this pattern of behavior is not in keeping with the ethical standards of our company, is a misuse of the First Amendment rights we cherish, and violates the spirit of tolerance we hold dear for people of all faiths and persuasions.

Please accept our sincerest apologies. I hope that trust in our company and its leadership can be restored.

Sincerely,

Ms. Mary Roe, Chairperson

Emotional Dissonance

As I typed these words, I had two conflicting emotions:

1. **Despair**—thinking that the probability of either of these two letters becoming a model for communication between Hollywood and people of faith was at the level of a blizzard over Hades' lake of fire.
2. **Euphoria**—thinking that, for the first time in the history of American entertainment, the kind of mutual respect and caring reflected in these two messages could actually happen, and a new wave of trust and honest, respectful dialogue could begin.

So, I believe in miracles. Not to do so, is to believe in nothing beyond ourselves, an unacceptable alternative. Creating messages like the above are not complex, but someone on both sides has to take the first step.

Simple Action Point to Remember

I once did a search of the teachings of Jesus to find out what principles He set forth in dealing with broken relationships. I was doing a lot of counseling at the time, and it seemed that knowing His teachings might be really practical for the many broken relationships I was facing in the lives of counselees.

In various passages of the New Testament, I discovered that Jesus provided direction for three kinds of interpersonal breaches:

1. You have something against another person (Mark 11:25).
2. Another person has something against you (Matthew 5:23, 24).
3. The other person has a moral failure which breaches the relationship (Matthew 18:15).

The directive in all three cases is exactly the same: TAKE THE INITIATIVE, AND GO TO THE PERSON! In an interpersonal breach, the burden is always on BOTH parties to take the initiative to resolve it by sitting down with the other person. The first one to do so receives God's favor. Refusing to take the initiative is becoming an accomplice to the offense that caused the breach in the relationship in the first place.

Letting a matter fester like an infection is to provide a breeding ground for bitterness and resentment. Harboring resentment and bitterness—my minister once noted—is like drinking rat poison and then waiting around for the rats to die. Forgiveness and good will clear the air in relationships and create a seedbed for luxuriant growth of mutual care and understanding.

Will Someone Hum a Line?

After the two lead characters in David Brandes' film *The Quarrel*, had argued passionately over faith for hours—arguments which, at one point, had each going his own way—a moment of humanity touched them. Chaim rebuked his Rabbi friend with "I needed a friend, not another angry voice." Hersh responded, "If Joseph and his brethren [who sold him into slavery] can make peace, Chaim, then so can we. This time, let's hear each other out."

Finally, exhausted from their stressful interchange, they sat in silence until one recalled the melody of a song they sang in Yeshiva as young men and began to hum it. As one remembered a line and the other another, soon they were humming, then singing together . . . then dancing to the melody. At the end of song, they embraced. This beautiful last scene in *The Quarrel* could happen between people of faith and leaders of global media—joining in a song of unity . . . and maybe even a dance.

The lyrics are written on every person's heart—not in our heads or memories—by the Spirit of God.

Will someone hum the first line?

Many years ago, Ben Cohen and Jerry Greenfield of Ben and Jerry's Ice Cream brand published a statement which said:

I DON'T MIND BEING A PEBBLE, IF I KNOW
I'M PART OF AN AVALANCHE.

My sentiments completely. If an avalanche of good will could begin to flow between America's moral conservatives and gatekeepers of the nation's entertainment and information industries, incredible good could be accomplished. Enlightened media could inspire, inform, edify, encourage, and heal billions around the planet. The vast resources of an additional 150 million people or more supporting rather than fighting the advancement of responsible media would be awe-inspiring.

However, without some "pebbles" beginning to roll toward the middle common ground, the incendiary relationship will continue.

Without someone putting in place more girders in the bridge across the chasm, it will remain too short to fulfill its purpose—linking the two sides.

That would be sad.

CHASM
ENDNOTES

Chapter One: Laying the Footers

1. "The Numbers," <http//www.the-numbers.comglossary.php>, January 15, 2011.

2. Charles Fleming, *High Concept: Don Simpson and the Hollywood Culture of Excess*, London: Bloomsbury Publishing, 1998, 5-6.

3. More Dogs, Inc., *More Dogs Than Bones*, 2000.

4. "U.S. Census Population Clock," U.S. and World Population Clocks Census Population Clock, <http://www.census.gov/main/www/pop-clock.html>, January 28, 2011.

5. "Religion in America," <en.wikipedia.org/wiki/religion_in_the_united_states>.

6. Ben Stein, *The View from Sunset Boulevard: America as Brought to You by the People Who Make Television*. New York: Doubleday, 1980, n.p.

Chapter Two: "You're Worthless, and I'm Not"

1. Robert W. Welkos and Ranwa Yehia, "Death to the U.S., but Not Films," *Los Angeles Times*, October 31, 2001, Web.

2. Welkos and Yehia.

3. Peter Bart, Editor of *Variety*, referred to evangelicals, for example, as "a bunch of know-nothing yahoos in the Bible Belt," 2.

4. Michael Weisskopf, *Washington Post*, February 1, 1993, 1.

5. Bernard Goldberg, *Bias*, Washington, D.C.: Regnery Publishing, Inc., 2002, 126-127.

6. Anna Greenberg and Jennifer Berktold, *Evangelicals in America*, Greenberg, Quinlan, and Roslan Research, 2004.

Chapter Three: "It's Just a *Movie!*"

1. Joel Siegal, Review of *The Last Temptation of Christ*, on ABC TV's "Good Morning America" in Larry W. Poland, *The Last Temptation of Hollywood*, Redlands, CA: Mastermedia International, Inc., 1988, 255.

2. "Taking It E.T.," <http://www.snopes.com/business/market/man-dms.asp>, February 21, 2011.

3. Norman Herr, "Television and Health," <http://www.csun.edu/science/health/docs/tv&health.html>, January 18, 2011.

4. "Sneaking into R-Rated Movies," <http://www.connectwithkids.com/tipsheet/printer/100630_movies.shtml>, February 21, 2011.

5. "Television and Health," <http://www.csun.edu/science/health/docs/tv&health.html>, January 18, 2011.

6. "Television and Health."

7. "From Radio to the Internet: Christian Broadcasting at 90," <http://www.prophecynewswatch.com2011/February16/1685.html>, February 21, 2011.

8. Joanne Brokaw, "Contemporary Christian Radio Second Most Popular Music Format in U.S.," <www.beliefnet.com>, March 11, 2013.

9. Joe Flint, "ABC News Correspondent Greenfield Tears Into Talk Shows," *Variety*, April 17-23, 1995, 31.

10. Flint, 31.

Chapter Four: "What Do You Mean, It's Wrong?"

1. "David Begelman," <http//en.wikipedia.org/wiki/david_begelman>, January 19, 2011.

2. David McClintock, *Indecent Exposure: A True Story of Hollywood and Wall Street*," New York: Harper Collins, 2002.

3. Nancy Griffin and Kim Masters, *Hit and Run: How Jon Peters and Peter Guber Took Sony for a Ride*, New York: Touchstone, 1997.

4. David Shaw, "Inhale. Lie. Exhale. Lie.," *Los Angeles Times*, February 13, 2001.

5. Shaw.

6. Shaw.

7. Dennis McDougal, *The Last Mogul: Lew Wasserman, MCA, and the Hidden History of Hollywood*, Cambridge: Da Capo Press, 2001.

8. Stanley Kramer, *Inherit the Wind,* Stanley Kramer Productions.

9. Michael Medved, "Hollywood's Three Big Lies About Media and Society," <http://www.independent.org/events/transcript/asp?eventID=69>, February 21, 2011.

10. "Survey and Market Research Findings in the United States," A Confidential Report Prepared for Mastermedia International, America's Research Group, March 2011, iii.

11. "How Many Words Are There in the English Language?," <http://www.oxforddictionaries.com/page/93>, January 20,1011.

12. Luke 6:45, *Holy Bible: New International Version*, 1984.

13. "We Have No Right to Happiness," *The Saturday Evening Post*, December, 1963, 21-28.

14. Brad Pitt, "Quotables," *World*, November 17, 2001, 11.

15. "Celebrity" written and recorded by American country music singer Brad Paisley. It was released in March 2003 as the lead single from his album, "Mud on the Tires."

16. E. Stanley Jones, *The Unshakable Kingdom and the Unchanging Person*," New York: Abingdon Press, 1972, 62-63.

Chapter Five: The Billy Maher Evangelistic Association

1. "Religulous—Vulgar and Blasphemous," <http://blogs.answersingenesis.org/blogs/ken-ham/2008/10/04/religulous—vulgar-and-blasphemous/>, January 24, 2011.

2. Neal Gabler, *Empire of Their Own: How Zukor, Laemmle, Fox, Mayer, Cohn and the Warner Brothers Invented Hollywood*, later changed to *An Empire of Their Own: How the Jews Invented Hollywood*, New York: Crown, 1988.

3. Joel Stein, "How Jewish is Hollywood?," <http://www.latimes.com/news/opinion/commentary/la-oe-stein19-2008dec19.0.7615084>, February 21, 2011.

4. "Bill Maher," <http://en.wikipedia.org/wiki/bill_maher>, January 11, 2011.

5. "Billy Ray Cyrus: Disney's 'Hannah Montana' Destroyed My Family," <http://www.hollywoodreporter.com/news/billy-ray-cyrus-disneys-hannah-99640>, February 15, 2011.

6. Rosie O'Donnell, *The View*, ABC Television, September 12, 2006.

Chapter Six: A Not-So-Ducky Episode

1. "Duck Dynasty's Phil Robertson Suspended By A&E Following Anti-Gay Comments," <http://www.accesshollywood.com>, December 18, 2013, n.p.

2. Jerry J. Gates, "How Many People Are Lesbian, Gay, Bisexual and Transgender?" Williams Institute, <http://www.williamsinstitute.law. ucla.edu/research/census-lgbt-demographics-studies>.

3. "WSJ's Riley, FNC's Williams Discuss 'Grievance Industry's Jesse Jackson's Entrance into 'Duck Dynasty' Controversy,'" www.breitbart.com, December 26, 2013, n.p.; "Jason Riley, Editorial Writer and Board Member of the *Wall Street Journal*: Interview with Juan Williams on O'Reilly Factor," December 26, 2013, <http://www.youtube. com/watch?v=aMzkPW_Y78g>.

4. Ben Urwand, *The Collaboration: Hollywood's Pact with Hitler*, Cambridge: Belknap Press of Harvard University Press, 2013, Book Jacket.

5. <http://www.youtube.com/watch?v=Y_OXS1vaX-M>.

Chapter Seven: Jesus Saves

1. "Brandon Tartikoff," <http://en.wikipedia.org/wiki/brandon-tartikoff>, January 26, 2011.

2. "Brandon Tartikoff Legacy Award," <http://www.natpe.org/conference/legacyawards>, January 2, 2011.

3. "Mindshare North America," WPP Group, 2008.

4. "The U.S. Religious Landscape Survey," The Pew Forum, 2008.

5. "Excerpt of Interview by Bill O'Reilly with Actress Patricia Heaton," <http://www.priestsforlife.org/media/heatonoreilly.htm>, October 1, 2002.

6. Fox Studio executive personal conversation with author.

7. *The Passion of the Christ*, Box Office Mojo, <http://boxofficemojo.com/movies/?id=passionofthechrist.htm>, January 26, 2009.

8. "NBC Broadcasts *Noah's Ark* Miniseries," <www.rae.org/nbcnoah.html>, May 15, 1999.

9. *The Book of Daniel* (TV Series), <http://en.wikipedia.org/wiki/the_book_of_daniel_(tv_series)>, January 26, 2011.

10. *The Book of Daniel*.

11. Unnamed screenwriter personal email to author.

12. "Cable News Ratings for Thursday, January 27, 2011; Piers Tumbles," <http:/tvbythenumbers.zap2it.com/2011/01/28/cable-news-ratings-for-thursday-january=27-2011-piers-tumbles/80643>, January 30, 2011.

13. Roger Ailes, email to author.

Chapter Eight: "Death to Conservatism!"

1. Penny Starr, "Screenwriter Says Hollywood Conservatives 'Have to Meet in Secret' and 'Talk in Whispers,'" <www.cnsnews.com/news/article/64745>, April 26, 2010.

2. Brent Baker, "Four Times More Journalists Identify as Liberal Than Conservative," quoting Pew Research Center, "Project for Excellence in Journalism," <http://newsbusters.org/blogs/brent-baker/2008/03/19/four-times-more-journalists-identify-liberal-conservative>, March 22, 2011.

3. Dennis Prager, "Liberalism and Conservatism: A Moral Comparison," Video and Audio CD, <www.dennisprager.com>.

4. "Paris Hilton Pleads Guilty in Cocaine Arrest," <http://www.latimes.com/entertainment/ktla-paris-hilton-plea-deal,0,6595520>, September 20, 2010.

5. "Star Trek," <http://www.snopes.com/inbocer/outrage/leave.asp>, February 3, 2011.

6. William Keck, "Celebrities Declare Own War—on Bush," *USA Today*, July 21, 2004.

7. Noel Sheppard, "Actor Jon Voight Blasts Nancy Pelosi, Democrats, and Anti-Bush Propagandists," <www.newsbusters.org/node/12633>, May 9, 2007.

8. *Fahrenheit 9/11*, <http://en.wikipedia.org/wiki/michael_moore>, February 8, 2011.

9. *The Handmaid's Tale* (1990), <http://www.imdb.com/title/tt0099731/>, February 8, 2011.

10. *The Handmaid's Tale*, <http://www.boxofficemojo.com/movies/?id=handmaidstale.htm>, February 8, 2011.

Chapter Nine: The Hef and Paris Factor

1. "Average and Median Sale Price for a New Home," <http://www.wsjprimerate.us/new_home_sales_price_history.htm>, February 8, 2011.

2. "Real Estate Home Appreciation—Last Twelve Months (Last Updated 2/3-2011)," <www.realestateabc.com/outlook/overall.htm>, February 8, 2011.

3. "Median Household Income," <en.wikipedia.org/wiki/median_household_income>, February 8, 2011.

4. Larry Rohter, "Mockery is Made of Disney Memo," *New York Times*, <http://query.nytimes.comgst/fullpage.htm>, February 12, 1991.

5. Lea Goldman and Tatiana Serafin, "The 20 Most Expensive Celebrity Weddings," <http://www.forbes.com/2007/07/12/celebrity-media-weddings-bz-media>, July 12, 2007.

6. "Plenty of Hideouts for Rupert Murdoch If Things Go Down Under," <http://curbed.com/archives/2011/01/25/plenty-of-hideouts-for-rupert-murdoch-should-things-go-down-under-1.php>, March 3, 2011.

7. "Watches" (Special Edition), *The Hollywood Reporter*, November/December, 2012, 70 pp.

8. "Boy Toys: Supercharged Watch," *The Hollywood Reporter*, January 10, 2012, 58.

9. William, "Busted. 100 Celebrities Arrested for Drug Possession," <www.popcrunch.com>, February 9, 2011; "Top 20 Drug-Induced Celebrity Deaths—Part I," <www.casapalmera.com>, February 9, 2011; "Famous Celebrities Who Have Been in Rehab," <www.drugalcohol-rehab.com/famous-addict.htm>, February 10, 2011.

10. "Megan Fox: 'Everyone in Hollywood Does Drugs,'" <http://www.hollywood.com/news>, July 7, 2007.

11. Charles Fleming, *Don Simpson and the Hollywood Culture of Excess*, 1998, London: Bloomsbury Publishing, 233.

12. Fleming, 234.

13. Fleming, 233.

14. Fleming, 256, 8.

15. Drew Pinsky and S. Mark Young, *The Mirror Effect: How Celebrity Narcissism is Seducing America*, New York: Harper Collins, 2009, 112-121.

16. Pinsky and Young.

17. "Paris Hilton," *Yahoo News*, July 17, 2006.

18. Pinsky and Young, 23-24.

19. Pinsky and Young, 15.

20. "Playboy Enterprises," <http://en.wikipedia.org/wiki/playboy_enterprises>, February 15, 2011.

Chapter Ten: "You Make No Sense!"

1. "Nancy Astor, Viscountess Astor," <http://en.wikipedia.org/nancy_astor,_viscountess_astor>, February 16, 2011.

2. "Disraeli and Gladstone: Opposing Forces," <http://www.bbc.co.uk/history/british/victorians/disraeli_gladstone_01.shtml>, February 17, 2011.

3. Joe Scarborough, MSNBC, "Why Is It Okay to Attack God and Christians?" <http://www.msnbc.msn.com/cleanprint/CleanPrintProxy.aspx?1297994731885>, February 17, 2011.

4. "Survey and Market Research Findings in the United States," A Confidential Report Prepared for Mastermedia International, America's Research Group, March 2011, vi.

5. "Doubting Darwin," *Time*, February 14, 2010, n.p.

6. Lydia Saad, "More Americans 'Pro-life' Than 'Pro-Choice' for First Time," <www.gallup.com/poll/118399/more-americans-pro-life-than-pro-choice-first-time.espx>, May 15, 2009, 1-6.

7. "Federal Laws that Protect Bald Eagles," <http://www.fws.gov/midwest/eagle/protect/laws.html>, March 7, 2011.

8. William Browning, "Barbara Bush Pro-Gay Marriage Stance Contrary to Father's Beliefs," <http://news.yahoo.com/s/ac/20110201/

pl_ac/7757395/_barbara_bush_progay_marriage_stance_contrary_
to_fathers_beliefs_1/>, February 1, 2011.

Chapter Eleven: "Shock and Awe"

1. "Boycott of Walt Disney: By the Southern Baptists," <http://www.
religioustolerance.org/disney4.htm>, February 24, 2011.

2. "Boycott of Walt Disney."

3. "Boycott of Walt Disney."

4. Donald E. Wildmon and Randall Nulton, *Don Wildmon: The Man
the Networks Love to Hate*, Anderson, Indiana: Bristol House Limited,
1990.

Chapter Twelve: "Don't You Know Who I Am?"

1. *Occupational Outlook Handbook, 2012 Edition, U.S. Bureau of Labor
Statistics*, <http://www.bls.gov/ooh/entertainment-and-sports/ac-
tors.htm>, January 18, 2014.

2. *Occupational Outlook Handbook*.

3. Pinsky and Young, 15.

4. "Barack Obama: Bitter Pennsylvanians 'Cling to Guns or Religion,'"
<http://inkslwc.wordpress.com/2008/04/12/barack-obama-bitter-
pennsylvanians-cling-to-guns-or-religion/>, March 20, 2011.

Chapter Thirteen: The Fulcrum

1. "Porgy and Bess," <http://en.wikipedia.org/wiki/Porgy_and_Bess>,
March 16, 2011.

2. George Gershwin, "It Ain't Necessarily So" Lyrics, <http://www.
stlyrics.com/songs/g/georgegershwin8836/itaintnecessarily-
so299755.html>, March 16, 2011.

3. Ann Coulter, *Godless: The Church of Liberalism*, New York: Crown Forum, 2006.

4. Joe Eszterhas, "Guest Voices: My Base Instincts and God's Love," *Washington Post*, September 9, 2008, <http://onfaith.washington-post.com/onfaith/guestvoices/2008/09/my_base_instincts_and_gods_love.html>, March 16, 2011.

5. Joe Eszterhas, *Cross Bearer: A Memoir of Faith*, New York: St. Martin's Press, 2008, Flyleaf.

6. Eszterhas, "Guest Voices."

7. Eszterhas, *Cross Bearer*.

8. "Survey and Market Research Findings in the United States," A Confidential Report Prepared for Mastermedia International, America's Research Group, March 2011, v.

Chapter Fourteen: "What? You're a Decent Human Being?"

1. *Lord Save Us From Your Followers* Website, <http://lordsaveusthe-movie.com/>, March 17, 2011.

2. Hollie McKay, "Critics Slam ABC Pilot 'Good Christian Bitches' for 'Inappropriate,' 'Damaging' Title," Published March 04, 2011, *FoxNews.com*. <http://www.foxnews.com/entertainment/2011/03/04/critics-slam-abc-pilot-good-christian-bitches-inappropriate-damaging-title/>, March 17, 2011.

3. Bryan Fischer, "Good Christian Bitches" Series Is a Hate Crime," <http://www.themoralliberal.com/2011/03/07/"good-christian-bitches"-series-is-a-hate-crime/>, March 9, 2011.

4. Brian Lowry, "Org Throws Up a Prayer for Media Moguls," *Variety*, October 6, 2004, 2.

CPSIA information can be obtained at www.ICGtesting.com
Printed in the USA
BVOW05s0611230514

354013BV00002B/6/P

9 781630 470623